From CATERPILLAR To *Butterfly*

From CATERPILLAR To Butterfly

Transform the Life You Have into the Life You Love

Charlene Dior Blandon

© 2017 Charlene Dior Blandon
All rights reserved.
ISBN: 0-9993737-0-6
ISBN 13: 978-0-9993737-0-5
Library of Congress Control Number: 2017914346
From Caterpillars to Butterflies, Houston, TX

For every person trapped inside a cocoon, longing to breakthrough and finally fly.

Contents

Introduction	9
1. Getting Real with Yourself about Yourself	17
2. You Are Meant to Transform	33
3. The Truth about Purpose	47
4. Be Content Where You Are	63
5. Change Your Frequency to Change Your Life	75
6. Expand Your Vision to Expand Your Life	89
7. Balance and Boundaries	105
8. Know Your Values	121
9. Manifest Your Heart's Desires	137
10. Be Powerful and Confident	151
11. Stay the Course	167
12. Rules for the Journey	181
13. Conclusion	195
Appendix: Worksheets and Exercises	201
Going Deeper	210
About Charlene	211

Introduction

Last night I went to bed
with setbacks running through my head.
Teardrops on my pillowcase, praying for a brighter day.
Joy comes in the morning. At least that's what they told me.
They should have left a warning,
That morning ain't tomorrow.
Because tomorrow is today. And nothing's really changed.
It looks a lot like yesterday.
Tomorrow is today. Everything's the same.
It feels a lot like yesterday.

I wrote these lyrics years ago. Life felt a little blah. Although I was pregnant with possibilities and hopeful for my future, I was stuck. I was so starved for meaning and fulfillment that I became spiritually emaciated. I've always been a dreamer and optimist. And now this bright-eyed, dreamy optimist was slowly turning into a negative, "life sucks" pessimist.

I was unhappy. I hated my job and my coworkers. I was single, overweight, and chronically tired. The one thing I had going for me, a budding real-estate portfolio, was becoming a bust and fast. I felt underwhelmed, underutilized, and unimportant.

As long as I can remember, I have always had this grandiose vision of what life would be. It is something that I held on to even in the bleakest of circumstances. And now for the first time in my life, my faith in my future plummeted.

No matter what I tried, I couldn't get unstuck. I couldn't get that fire back. I couldn't transform my life the way I most wanted to. The shackles of despair and disappointment had a tight grip on me, and they were getting tighter. This was new to me. I had always been able to wiggle my way free from confining moments in my life. I had always been able to find the air bubble so I could breathe, if only just a little. Yet here I was suffocating.

On the surface I was miserable. I felt tricked and misled by God Himself. I was hurt and faithless. Yet somewhere deep inside I just knew that this couldn't be all that there was to life. I just couldn't have reached the pinnacle of my days. I knew that there was something else available to me, and I shouldn't settle for where I was.

One day I was at the bookstore in the coffee section. I used to go to the bookstore and just read books and take notes. I had embarked on a personal growth journey. I was committed to learning more about myself and the principles of life. Out of the corner of

Introduction

my eye, as I looked up briefly to reflect on something I had just read, I saw it.

It was a coffee mug for sale that said, "Just when the caterpillar thought its world was over, it became a butterfly." That quote spoke to my soul.

I thought, "Oh my goodness, I think I am becoming a butterfly. My world isn't over. I have been stuck inside this cocoon, and it's time for me to break out of it."

I think that butterflies are such an inspiring example for us. If God created the creepy, crawly caterpillar to transform into the beautiful, adorned butterfly, what does He have in store for you and me? Butterflies are an example that we're supposed to grow. We're meant to transform and improve. They show us that there is something else more beautiful in store for us if we are willing to embrace our growth opportunities.

A lot of times, we avoid growth. We make statements such as these:

"I was like this when they met me."
"I was like this when he married me."
"I was like this when she hired me."

We say these things to give ourselves permission to stay the same. We say that we are just "keeping it one hundred." This is so crazy. If you don't know that you have to grow, you are in for a lifetime of dissatisfaction, unfulfillment, and mediocrity. You totally have to grow!

We often hesitate to grow because we feel that if we acknowledge that we have a growth opportunity, we are admitting that we are flawed or inadequate in some way.

Years ago in my first job out of college, I was in my director's office. He said to me, "Charlene, do you need help with networking?"

I said, "Well, yeah. Everybody does."

The truth was that networking and conversing with people I did not know made me cringe. It still does at times.

I made it okay to admit networking was a weakness for me by saying that "everybody does." I felt somewhat safe admitting that networking was one of my growth opportunities by saying that it was the same growth opportunity for everyone else. I was embarrassed to say that networking was a weakness for me and that I had room to grow in this area. I didn't want to admit that I wasn't good enough.

Nobody wants to admit that he or she is not good enough because the truth is we fight those thoughts on our own anyways. We do not want to start speaking it out loud to other people, and so we tend to stay the same. We stay stuck because we cannot acknowledge or appreciate that growth is natural. It is beautiful. Yet we will divorce so that we can avoid growing. We will lose romantic relationships, friendships, and career opportunities. We will miss out on anything and everything just to avoid growing.

Because, you know? "I've been like this. I'm keeping it one hundred."

That is not the right attitude. I believe that we are meant to grow just as the caterpillar transforms into the beautiful butterfly. The interesting thing is that there is purpose in being a caterpillar. There's purpose in every stage of that life cycle. A caterpillar's focus and job is to eat. If the caterpillar does not eat enough, it will not survive the cocoon. There will never be a butterfly. So a caterpillar has a specific, critical purpose to fulfill. There is nothing wrong with being a caterpillar just like there is nothing wrong with being the current you. There is nothing wrong with

Introduction

the current Charlene, but there is something wrong with staying the current Charlene. There is something wrong with staying a caterpillar because a caterpillar has a much more beautiful future in store. We don't have to look at our current situation as us not being good enough. We do have to know, accept, and acknowledge that we just can't stay here.

Life has this crazy tendency to knock us down. We have setbacks, unfair situations, and heartbreaking events. We have dreams deferred, confining years, and times when we give more than we receive. When these unfortunate things happen, we tend to think, "Woe is me." Yet it's not "Woe is me." It's "Grow is me." The times when life feels as if it is picking on us, we have the choice to crumble in the experience or to grow through the experience. Life wants us to choose growth.

I believe the purpose of life is to grow—spiritually, mentally, physically, emotionally, financially. We always have to be growing so that we can live up to our fullest potential. Our goals and dreams evolve throughout our lifetimes. In order to always accomplish what we want to accomplish—our newest goals and visions—we always have to be growing. We have to be committed to advancing and improving ourselves continuously so that we can give our greatest contributions and experience all that is there for us to experience in this life. Personal growth has to be a lifestyle.

My experience drew me into wanting to grow, because I didn't want to live my whole life in a perpetual funk. There was no other solution. I had to grow or settle. I wasn't settling.

FROM CATERPILLAR TO BUTTERFLY

Sometimes life will bring us along to make us grow. Other times we have to grow to bring life along. In other words, when life gets stuck and stagnant, sometimes we have to move first. We have to grow to get life to go where we want it to go.

I honestly believe that everything that we could possibly want is within reach. We just have to be willing to grow. That means being committed to learning things that you don't already know and overcoming the limiting beliefs that you hold that impact your life. It means being exposed to new ideas, new people, and new concepts. It means being willing to invest your time and your money into yourself.

There's always a gap between where you are and where you want to be. Sometimes we judge the gap. We let the gaps tell us that we're inferior or that we are not capable of accomplishing certain things. We let the gap define our self-worth. But the truth of the matter is that as long as you are alive, you will have a gap. If you are fully alive and fully present in this thing called life, you will have a gap. So it's nothing to judge. It's just to acknowledge. Be able and willing to close the gaps. The way that you close the gap is by growing.

When I started investing in myself, in personal growth, I realized the impact that it had on my life. It had an impact on the way I felt about myself. It had an impact on the way that I felt about life itself. It had an impact on what I thought I was capable of doing, achieving, and receiving. It made a remarkable difference for me and the way that I lived my life. I embarked on this journey, and I saw firsthand what personal growth could do. I became passionate about sharing this newfound knowledge with other people.

Introduction

And that's what led to being a coach, the website fromcaterpillarstobutterflies.com, and now this book.

This book is all about growth. It holds the tools and techniques that I learned in my quest to transform the life I had into the life I love. I share practical insights that you can begin to implement into your life immediately. You'll also find Getting Real questions throughout the book. These questions are designed to help you apply what you've learned in each chapter. They are also designed to aid you in reflecting on your life—the good, the bad, and the ugly—so you can grow. Don't skip over this section. When you search inside yourself for answers, something majestic happens. Transformation happens. This is an important part of the journey.

I admire you for picking up this book. I can tell you are serious about your transformation. It is my hope that as a result of reading this book and applying the concepts, your life will never be the same.

Sometimes small change seems insignificant. Yes, this is just a book. Yet you never know what impact something as small as a book, a chapter, or even one sentence can have on your life. Once you've learned something, whether about yourself or life, you cannot unlearn it. There's no such thing as ungrowing. Once a caterpillar becomes a butterfly, she never goes back to being a caterpillar again.

1 Getting Real with Yourself about Yourself

Growth and transformation are hard. They are "get all up in your face and call you out unapologetically" hard. There's this mix of fear, insecurity, embarrassment, shame, and pain that sprout up when you want to push through current circumstances. They are the black box of transformation that most people want to avoid.

Yet on the other side of all that muck is something beautiful. Your growth, your transformation, is beautiful. You just have to get to the other side.

Getting to the other side requires your courage. It requires your heroic honesty. It might even ask of you tears, emotional upset, and heartbreak. But in return it gives you peace of mind, a powerful sense of self, and an unstoppable resolve that makes life beautiful.

Own the Role You Play

I often ask women on our coaching calls, "What role have you played in the way your life has unfolded?"

Sometimes after a contemplative pause, a woman might murmur, "I don't know."

The truth is you've played a role. We all have. Of course life happens. Of course people do things that hurt us or that have a profound effect on who we are. Yet in the midst of all the external influences, there is still a role that we all play in our lives.

If you can't acknowledge this truth, you're not ready to transform your life. Nor are you ready to embrace this book fully. You might as well throw it out now. Growth requires confrontation. The scariest confrontation of all is sometimes the one we have with ourselves.

Get past the idea that life, God, or another person is somehow to blame for where you are at this point in your journey. For if it is life's fault, how do you persuade or coerce her to release the shackles of disappointment, unfulfillment, and despair from you? You cannot bully life into submission. Life is not afraid of you. You are afraid of life.

If it is God's fault, what prayer can you pray that is different from the hundreds of other prayers you have undoubtedly prayed that would convince Him of your worthiness to be blessed beyond measure? And how do you reconcile the truth that He is no respecter of people? What He has done for someone else He can do for you as well.

And if it is someone else's fault, how do you give sight to the blind who do not know that he or she is blind? How do you show someone the errors of his or her ways when he or she does not want to see? How do you convince a broken, hurt, and soulfully deceased person that he or she is wrong and should take it back?

"They should take it back." Take what back exactly? The implication is that you are holding in your hands a bloody, bruised, depressed heart. You want somebody—God, life, anybody—to take the lifeless, broken heart you are holding. You are searching for someone to blame so that he or she might take the scarred heart from your hands.

Yet you cannot live without a heart. The idea is not to give away your heart—your power. The idea is to heal and grow. You cannot heal or grow what you have given away.

There's no one to blame. The only person who matters in this moment is you. You cannot control anyone but yourself. You cannot control life or God. You have to own the role that you have played and the role that you will play in how your life unfolds in the future.

In other words what decisions led you to this point in your life? What actions and inactions on your part got you here? What decisions and actions are you prepared to take to reshape your future?

When you own the role you've played in the movie of your life, you can rewrite the script. You can make better decisions, switch up the roles, and change out the characters.

As my high-school chemistry teacher used to say, "You have the power of the pen."

Be Responsible for Your Responsibilities

Life is full of responsibilities. The blessings that are bestowed upon us come ripe with them. The roles we play as wives, mothers, daughters, and professionals are all our responsibilities.

We know how to be responsible when it counts. You show up to work rain or shine. You carry out your work duties daily and on time, if only barely. You bite your tongue when your boss offends you. Your work responsibilities are delivered to you in a nice package with a big pretty bow on it called a paycheck.

What if you took that same attitude and applied it to your other life responsibilities? What if you showed up to life rain or shine? What if you carried out your life, health, money, and relationship duties daily and on time? What if you bit your tongue when your spouse offended you?

One of the reasons our lives fall apart is because we haven't been responsible for our responsibilities. You have a responsibility to every area of your life. You cannot ignore your responsibilities away. They are always there. This is where a lot of people get into trouble and create discord in their lives. They neglect their responsibilities.

Sometimes people neglect their responsibilities because they do not see them as responsibilities. All of life's blessings, big or small, are propelled to responsibility like a magnet. You cannot have one without the other. If you try to accept the blessing without the responsibility, the blessing will disintegrate. If you harbor the responsibility without the blessing, the weight of it will crush you.

If you have a responsibility that you neglect, it will deteriorate. Sometimes we push the limits on how long we can neglect something before it becomes a problem. In the back of our minds, we know we should be paying attention to that thing. Just one more day and we'll get to it. But then suddenly there are no more days. The thing we have neglected falls apart before our eyes. When this happens some people will mourn the loss, confused as to how it came to be about. Deep down they're not confused. They know exactly what happened. They weren't being responsible.

Responsibility can be paralyzing. Sometimes you're paralyzed by fear. You wonder if you're capable of handling the responsibility. Other times, you're paralyzed by goals held in bondage. You resent the compromise required between responsibility and dreams. We've all heard the stories of mothers who abandon their newborns and fathers who walk out of their families never to return again. While most of us would never do anything that extreme we have our own ways of avoiding responsibility. In due time that avoidance catches up with us, particularly when we lose something we wanted to keep.

No one is exempt from responsibilities. The problem is we don't always own those responsibilities. At times we don't want to be responsible because it feels like a burden. Being responsible can be intimidating. It can be stressful and inconvenient. It can require too much time and too much money. It can require sacrifice.

It seems easier just to skip out on responsibility.

You have to be responsible for your responsibilities. They should give you a sense of pride and gratitude. I can ensure you that someone wants your blessings even with the responsibility. Responsibility is not a curse. It is the gateway for which all the things we want out of life are received.

If your life, marriage, finances, or another area is falling apart, assess how responsible you've been in that area. Ask yourself, "Where do I need to be more responsible?"

Being irresponsible costs you something. If you are irresponsible with your job—you show up late, you don't go in at all, you don't complete your assignments on time—you will be fired.

That same principle is applied to all of life. If you are not responsible for your responsibilities, you will be relieved of said responsibilities. If you do not own that you are responsible, it's never going to work out. Your relationships will not work out. Your finances will not work out. Your dreams will not work out.

One of the ways you can get real with yourself about yourself and own the role you have played in your life's unfoldment is to acknowledge the times and places you have been irresponsible.

Perhaps you didn't realize that there was a set of responsibilities that came with that blessing. Maybe you knew there were responsibilities, but you didn't know exactly what they were. Maybe you knew what they were, but you didn't know how to fulfill them. Maybe you were just being irresponsible.

The reason doesn't really matter. What matters now is that you identify those areas and learn how to be responsible so that you can do better the next time.

How to Be Responsible

GAINS is an acronym that explains what it means to be responsible. As you read through this section, reflect on the responsibilities you have. Pay attention to how responsible you are across all areas of your life and if you have room to improve.

Give: When you're responsible for a thing, you give it what it needs. You give food, clothes, and shelter to the children you are responsible for. You give time, energy, and effort to the job you are responsible for.

Attend: That for which you are responsible requires your attention on a consistent basis. The same way that you would not leave your job unattended for weeks at a time is the same way you should not neglect to give your attention for weeks at a time to the marriage or the body for which you are responsible.

Intent: You are intentional about what you are responsible for. People who are fiscally responsible are intentional about how they earn, spend, and save money.

Notice: You own your responsibilities by being observant. You notice how things are or are not progressing. You notice what is or is not working so that you can adjust.

Stay: Lastly you stay committed to fulfilling your responsibilities. You don't quit halfway through. You don't back out of your commitments. Being responsible also means finishing what you started.

When you accept and appreciate the responsibilities that come with your blessings, your "have to" will transcend into "I'm honored to."

If you cannot manage the responsibilities of your current life, you will struggle with managing the responsibilities of your dream life. Get responsible now.

Let Your Yes Mean Yes

I can't count how many times someone has said yes to working with me further as their coach, yet when it was time to make the financial investment, they ignored my e-mails and phone calls. Their yes didn't really mean yes.

If your yes doesn't mean yes, I can almost guarantee that your no doesn't really mean no either. In other words when you halfheartedly say yes to your dreams, your future, your peace of mind, your self-discovery, your health, and so on, what you are really saying is, "Meh, I could go either way on that."

And when you say no to those things that don't align with who you are and where you want to go, you really mean "Whatever you want to do works for me." Your line in the sand is easily washed away by the slightest wave.

When your yes doesn't mean yes and your no doesn't mean no, you're not honoring yourself. You're confusing life. You're confusing God. You're confusing your hopes and dreams. You can't transform your life in such a confused state.

Your yes/no muscle has to be strong to create a life you love. Like building any muscle, this is a process. You will learn some tips throughout this book that will help you strengthen this muscle. The most important thing is to acknowledge if this is a problem for you and where it shows up in your life.

Your yes/no muscle is weak because you're plagued with doubts and fears.

"What if I'm making a mistake?"
"What if it's not the right path?"
"What if I need the money later?"
"What if they get mad at me?"

When your doubts and fears are stronger than your dreams and desires, your yes/no muscle is weak. You say yes but you mean no because you're afraid. You say no when you mean yes also because you are afraid.

My yes/no muscle is weakest when it comes to financial decisions. I had an opportunity to work with a business coach. The investment was $10,000, by far the most I had ever invested in a coach. My heart was racing. "What should I do?" I wondered.

People always say, "Feel the fear, and do it anyway." I find that saying to be quite funny. Which fear are you talking about? When I was presented with the opportunity to work with this coach, I had two fears—the fear of missing out (on a life-changing opportunity) and the fear of losing out (on my money).

I didn't know what to do. Getting the money together wasn't a problem. I had it. The question was, did I want to give it?

I walked to the park across the street from the hotel where the event was being held. My heart was pounding so fast it nearly jumped out of my chest.

Contrary to the storm brewing inside my mind, it was a beautiful day. The sun was shining. The sky was a magnificent blue. People were out and about, laughing, playing sports, and sitting in the shade enjoying the weather.

I took a seat on a park bench under the shade of a large tree. I wanted to sit alone quietly. I needed to think. I wanted to talk to God. I needed His direction.

I inhaled deeply and closed my eyes. "God, give me a sign. Order my steps."

I was hoping for some extraordinary, magical moment. Perhaps the sky would break open and God Himself would call out to me, "Charlene, this is the path in which you should take."

But that didn't happen, and I had a deadline. I had to make a decision soon. I couldn't breathe. I cried. I prayed. I meditated. Still no miraculous moment occurred. Still I had to make a decision before the deadline hours later.

The truth was I knew what I wanted to do. Of course, if something has the chance to change my life and my business, I'm all in. But my doubts and fears were all in as well. They almost won the battle, but in the end my dreams and desires won out. I invested in that coach.

Sometimes your yes is in your heart and your no is in your head. Your heart is pulled to those things that set it on fire. Your brain is analytical. It searches for facts and figures, deductive reasoning, and sound projections. Your brain wants to know that one plus one equals two. If it can't figure out how to make the math work, it serves up a million reasons why you should second-guess your heart.

In all honesty I wanted assurances that this would be a sound investment. I wanted to know the future. I wanted to be certain that I would not be losing out on my money. If I could just see into the future, I would know what I should do today. Unfortunately, seeing the future is not a skill set I have.

When you want to strengthen your yes/no muscle, you have to be courageous enough to give your own assurances. Not the assurance that the decision you're making will result in the returns you are expecting. You are assuring yourself that whatever happens you are capable of turning it into something beautiful. You are assuring yourself that you have your best interests at heart and that you would never purposefully lead yourself astray. You are assuring yourself that God is with you here and in your future.

Other times your yes isn't really a yes because you don't know how to tell your truth. You lack the self-confidence to be honest with yourself and others. You tell people what they want to hear.

Sometimes the person you want to be says yes, but the person you are now is not ready for yes.

Acknowledging your incongruences is an important part of getting real with yourself about yourself. When you're incongruent, you don't really stand for what you stand for. You don't really believe what you believe in.

Let your yes be yes and your no be no. Your yes/no muscle is a powerful tool that will help you transform the life you have into the life you want.

Unscrew the Screw-Up

FROM CATERPILLAR TO BUTTERFLY

Let's face it—at one point or another, we all screw up. Yes, everybody. What happens a lot of the times is we screw up and then we walk away. There's an attitude of "Oh well, I screwed that up" or "Everything happens for a reason."

Creating a life you love requires that you unscrew your screw-ups. You don't just leave your mess in the middle of the floor never to return to face it again. When you refuse to address your mess, you leave a trail of screw-ups behind you. You can play connect the dots with the screw-ups that led you to where you are today.

One of the reasons we walk away from our screw-ups is because we don't want to acknowledge that we did in fact screw that up. It's easier to walk away and "start fresh" than it is to attempt to clean up the mess.

The problem is that life is full of screw-ups. If you don't ever empower yourself to unscrew them, you'll always be running from one mess to another.

You have to get real with your screw-ups. Don't keep sweeping them under the rug. Don't keep walking away from them. Own that you have in fact screwed up, and where there is opportunity, work to unscrew your screw-ups.

This could mean making an apology. Repair a relationship you screwed up. This could mean getting out of debt and repairing the credit you screwed up. It could mean getting training to jump-start the career or business you screwed up.

Stop leaving a pile of screw-ups in your path. Do what you can to clean up your mess, learn from your mistakes, and improve your future.

Getting Real with Yourself about Yourself

If you want to transform your life, you can't hide behind a mask. I used to tell an ex-boyfriend, "You can lie to me, but you can't lie to yourself." He was a habitual liar, and I grew exhausted trying to analyze and confront all of his lies.

Going through life wearing a mask gets exhausting. Trying to lie to yourself and everyone else gets exhausting. Trying to convince yourself that you are the victim and have played no role in your own life's unfoldment gets tiresome. Trying to convince yourself that you don't want what you want and that you're okay with the life you have, is draining. It leaves you powerless. It leaves you confined. It leaves you unfulfilled.

The truth will set you free. Not most of the truth. Partial truths will stifle your transformation. The whole truth. Almost truthful doesn't count. Are you brave enough to face your unaltered truths? You will have a chance on the next page to tell your truth.

𝒯he Beautiful 𝒯ruth

This chapter might seem a little harsh. I've challenged you to get real about your faults, irresponsibleness, incongruences, and screw-ups. It's what I have to do as a coach. I told you growth and transformation would get all up in your face. Your transformation requires a confrontation.

Yet I would be remiss if I did not acknowledge that there are some amazingly beautiful truths about you as well. It's beautiful that you still believe in possibilities. You're still here. You're still standing. You're still giving yourself a chance to create a life you love.

It's beautiful that you've fallen and gotten back up again. Your willingness to stare growth and transformation in the eyes and not back down is beyond beautiful.

No matter what's "wrong" in your life right now, I know that there are some beautiful "rights" as well. And I know that you've played a role in that.

The beautiful truth is that you are courageous. You are someone who doesn't simply wish. You are a doer.

I'd venture to say you've shown strength in ways that have astonished yourself. You found hope in the hopelessness. You've given light to the dark. You are amazing in ways I'll likely never know.

There's a messy truth and a beautiful truth. Beautiful truth kicks messy truth's butt every day of the week. The messy truth will set you free. The beautiful truth will give you wings so that you might fly.

Getting Real

What role have you played in the way your life has unfolded up until this point?

_____
_____
_____

Is your yes/no muscle weak? When is it weakest? When is it strongest?

_____

Getting Real with Yourself about Yourself

_____
_____

Have you not been the most responsible with your responsibilities? Which ones? Why?

_____
_____
_____

Is it possible that you are where you are in life in part because you left a mess somewhere in your past? Where? Maybe you were too prideful or too ashamed to fix it. Have you made a habit of leaving your screw-ups screwed up?

_____
_____
_____

What's your beautiful truth?

_____
_____
_____

2 You Are Meant to Transform

In the last chapter, I told you it was time to get real with yourself about yourself. The truth will set you free. It might also leave you discouraged, sad, and in despair. That's a great place to be. You are ripe for a transformation.

The purpose of life is to grow. We're meant to grow physically, mentally, emotionally, spiritually, and financially. We're just not meant to stay the same. Knowing that you are meant to transform marks your past as inconsequential. It's no longer the scarlet letter you've been wearing on your heart. That's the old you, the caterpillar you.

I believe God put the caterpillar here on earth to teach us that we are not supposed to stay the same.

FROM CATERPILLAR TO BUTTERFLY

In the introduction I shared there is purpose in every stage of the caterpillar, and so there is purpose in every season we find ourselves in. There is purpose in every season you have found yourself in the midst of, and there is purpose in every season that has yet to come.

A caterpillar/butterfly creature has four distinct stages in their life cycle. First they're eggs. They are dropped on a plant by their mother. They are so small you would not likely notice them. A few days later they hatch, and out comes a caterpillar.

Eat and Grow

The main purpose of a caterpillar is to eat and grow. Caterpillars eat and eat and eat so that they can grow and grow and grow. They eat, and they grow.

Note that they are eating a lot to facilitate their massive growth. They don't just grow haphazardly. They have to eat to grow. When you are ready to grow, you have to feed yourself something. You too have to eat.

Sometimes life will pick the dish for you. We have all experienced life picking our dish. When life picks the dish for us, a lot of times it doesn't taste good. It tastes like licorice mixed with anchovies. It's the heartaches, the divorces, and the misfortunes that life serves up.

But most of the time I would argue we get to pick our dish. You get to pick what you will feed on to grow. But you've got to eat. What are you going to choose?

Sitting at my mom's house, I noticed the news playing on the television screen.

"Why are you watching that?" I asked.

"Why not? You don't watch the news?" she replied.

"Nope. God doesn't give us a spirit of fear, but the news does!" I proclaimed.

I don't watch the news. I can't. As an empath disasters and tragedies weigh heavily on my spirit. If I feed on the news, my fears grow. I choose to feed on those things that grow my faith.

Be mindful of what you are feeding on. Make sure it enables you to grow in a way that serves you well. Choose dishes that grow your faith, your confidence, your self-worth, and anything else that puts you and your future at an advantage.

Shed

A caterpillar grows so fast that it sheds its skin five times within two weeks.[1] Five times it sheds its skin and replaces it with new skin because its body keeps outgrowing the previous layer.

You will have to shed some things in your journey of transformation. Stop thinking you don't have to give anything up. You're going to have to shed people and habits. You might have to shed spending habits, eating habits, or thought habits. You're going to have to give up some behaviors, some friends, and some beliefs.

You will have to discard useless, prohibitive aspects of your life to grow. You might even have to shed more than once. This is where we get tripped up. We have a breakthrough moment—a breakthrough in mindset or a habit. Then we think we're good. We

---

[1] "Caterpillar growth and change: Complete Metamorphosis life cycle study pictures", Lifecycle Oneness Becomes Us, http://lifecycle.onenessbecomesus.com/larvae.html

think, "I just had this breakthrough. Bring on the good life."

Yet we don't realize that sometimes we need another breakthrough. You're not done yet. The first breakthrough was great. But you've got to shed some more. You need another season of shedding. This book might be your breakthrough, but you will likely need an additional breakthrough to follow.

I've always been a little on the shy side. In class I never raised my hand to answer a question even when I knew what the answer was. I didn't want to be the center of attention. Because of that it has always taken me a bit longer to develop relationships but when I did they were solid friendships.

As I entered into college and even into corporate America, my shyness presented bigger and bigger impediments. It took me even longer to develop close relationships. Not only did my personal life suffer; my career did as well. Colleagues often took me as unknowledgeable. They thought I didn't say a lot because I didn't know a lot.

Ultimately I came to a place where I no longer wanted my shyness to hold me back. I purposefully sought to enhance my self-confidence and overcome my reluctance to be seen. I joined Meetup, a site where strangers meet other individuals with similar interests and connect in person. I read books on confidence. I listened to guided meditations geared to build confidence. I pushed myself to say more in meetings. I pushed myself to be seen and heard.

I had a breakthrough in my confidence levels, and the results were liberating. I stopped worrying so much about doing or saying the wrong thing. I developed deeper relationships with friends and coworkers. I eased more into myself in my personal and professional lives. I ventured into real-estate investing. That takes some confidence. In general, my confidence was growing and my life reflected that growth.

Fast-forward a few years later and once again I feel stuck in my career. My peers were hop skipping over me on the corporate ladder. People with less experience, education, and skill were advancing quicker than I was.

"What is this about?" I often wondered, plagued by what I was doing wrong.

My introspection led me to the realization that I was still holding back. I still hesitated to share an idea or make a suggestion. I was still reluctant to take the bulls by the horn. My confidence was holding me back once again.

While I had broken through one ceiling years prior, there was now another confidence ceiling hindering me. I needed another breakthrough.

You might need another breakthrough after your last breakthrough. Don't stop at the first breakthrough. There could be two, three, four, or five more times you will be required to shed some things before you are really ready for the next stage.

Build Your Own Cocoon

When the caterpillar is ready to move on to the next season, it finds a secure spot. Let me repeat that. The caterpillar finds a secure spot to grow. When you're ready to grow, you can't grow just anywhere. You can't grow around just any ol' body. You have to grow in a secure spot.

That's why I love personal growth events. They are a secure spot. If you tell someone your wildest, biggest dream or vision at a personal growth event, that person is not going to look at you as though you're crazy. The person will not hate on you. That someone will not put seeds of doubt in you. The person is going to celebrate you and say, "That is awesome. Go for it."

That's why I am also a fan of coaching and masterminding. I've worked with a life coach. I've worked with a business coach and a fitness coach. Coaching relationships and masterminds have been a secure spot for me to transform.

Again, a caterpillar finds a secure spot to build its cocoon. You too have a build your cocoon in a safe place.

As I was researching this process, I came across a quote that sums up the impetus for all transformations. It said, "As time goes by, the caterpillar feels ever increased promptings and restlessly moves about.[2]

I don't imagine that someone tells the caterpillar it's time for it to build a cocoon. The mom does not come back and say, "Hey, little caterpillar babies, it's time for you guys to build a cocoon now."

The caterpillar feels promptings. It is as if there is someone pulling the caterpillar by this invisible rope saying, "Come this way."

Have you ever felt life pulling and tugging at you saying, "Come this way"? Perhaps it was the tug that led you to purchase this book.

Have you ever felt your feet moving and not really knowing where they were going? You

---

[2] "Caterpillar growth and change: Complete Metamorphosis life cycle study pictures", Lifecycle Oneness Becomes Us, http://lifecycle.onenessbecomesus.com/larvae.html

want to stop. You yell to life, "Life, stop pulling me along." You end up bloody and bruised as you are dragged by the vision that delays and stalls as if it wants to taunt you.

Yet there is still an invisible pull at you telling you it's time. It's time for you to go to the next stage. "Keep going," life whispers back.

You are just like the caterpillar. You will get restless and uneasy. There will be a stirring in your soul. You'll be inclined to ignore it. Perhaps you already have. Thankfully the prompting isn't easily deterred. It returns again and again. It's the same instinctive nature of the caterpillar that tells you it's time for you to go to the next evolution. That same instinctive spirit or voice is inside of you too. It's advising you when it's time to go so that you might grow. It looks like being stuck. It looks like being restless. It looks like being unfulfilled. You have to learn to walk in blind faith when life starts to pull at you.

Metamorph

Once securely tucked inside of a cocoon of transformation, metamorphosis begins. This is a season of both increase and decrease simultaneously. The caterpillar almost completely digests itself. In place of the old tissues and features, new eyes, new legs, and of course wings start to grow.[3]

---

[3] Jabr, Ferris. "How Does a Caterpillar Turn into a Butterfly?" Scientific American. August 10, 2012. Accessed May 27, 2017.
https://www.scientificamerican.com/article/caterpillar-butterfly-metamorphosis-explainer/.

The mouth of the caterpillar changes. Caterpillars chew leaves, but butterflies sip nectar from flowers. The new creature that is emerging now has a straw-like tongue.[4]

The way that you used to do things, how you used to eat, or how you used to get around is changing. You're metamorphosing into something else during this season of your life, and you need new tools. You need new utensils. You need new direction because if you can fly, you can probably go a little further, a little faster, than if you're crawling. You need a new map during this stage. That's the purpose of the cocoon. It is to actually transform and metamorphose the caterpillar into a new creature.

This stage can last from seven days to a year. It's really important to acknowledge the time it takes caterpillars to transform, because your transformation is yours. You can't compare it to someone else's. You can't think, "Oh, it's taking me six months, and it's only taken her six days."

Everyone's growth is different just like every butterfly is different. It can take however long it needs to take for you to become the masterpiece that you're developing into. Don't compare yourself and your time line to someone else's.

Finally a beautiful butterfly emerges. Within a few hours, she is ready to fly. She flies into the vast blue sky and searches for a mate to start the process all over again.

Let's Recap

Here is a recap of the stages or seasons of transformation:

---

[4] https://www.joyfulbutterfly.com/what-do-caterpillars-eat/

You Are Meant to Transform

- 🦋 <u>A season of birth</u>: Beyond a physical birth, there are dreams and goals born in this season.
- 🦋 <u>A season of growth</u>: Baby dreams grow up and become big dreams. Baby confidence becomes adult confidence. Infant mind-sets and habits become mature mind-sets and habits.
- 🦋 <u>A season of transformation</u>: The old fades away as the new springs forth. Notice how growth comes before transformation. You may have to grow yourself before your life transforms.
- 🦋 <u>A season of flight and rest</u>: In this season you are reaching new heights and resting in the beauty of the masterpiece you have become.

Once the cycle is complete, ever growing we lay new eggs (that is new goals) and start the process all over again. You must continuously transform and grow. That is what you are designed to do so that you can be sure you reach your highest potential.

A lot of times people are so reluctant and afraid to do that very thing. How do you know that you've been afraid to grow? You've been unwilling to change. You have let some things go because you don't want to be different.

Imagine you walked outside your house and there were hundreds of dead caterpillars laid in the street. What would you think?

You'd probably look at those dead caterpillars and think, "What a shame. Those caterpillars never had the chance to be all that they can be. They sure did miss out. If they only knew."

You'd probably pull out your phone and take pictures of all the dead caterpillars.

FROM CATERPILLAR TO BUTTERFLY

You'd upload the pictures of the unfortunate creatures on social media and tell the whole world, "Look at these dead caterpillars. Look at these hundreds of caterpillars who missed their potential, who never got to make it to the masterpiece that was in store for them."

Your friends would leave sad-face emojis with the lone tear on your post because they too knew when someone didn't reach their full potential, it was heartbreaking.

Yet sometimes we are those caterpillars dead on the street. We just don't know it. And when we refuse to grow, we can pretty much count on becoming the equivalent.

The caterpillar doesn't know that she is going to become a butterfly. No one comes to tell her. She just feels the prompting in her soul that it's time to move on. She knows that it's time to build a cocoon and time to grow.

The caterpillar doesn't know what's on the other side of that cocoon. She might even be scared to be in that dark cocoon, confined. If she could talk, you'd perhaps hear her say, "I used to walk around in the sunlight. Now I'm stuck inside this cocoon with no light."

She doesn't even know how beautiful she is becoming, but she still follows the promptings in her heart. And she reaches her final destiny.

You don't know what's in store for you. Sometimes we want to know, and we get stuck because we're waiting to know. But you don't know because no one comes to tell you. No one comes to tell any of us. You have to follow the promptings in your heart so that you don't end up like the dead caterpillar in the street who missed her purpose and potential.

You Are Meant to Transform

You are meant to grow. You are meant to transform. You were not put here on this earth to stay the same. So when you get restless, when you feel the prompting, when you have the instinct to grow, you should grow. There are probably some things in your life and in your heart right now that you know you are not following through on.

There are some areas of your life that are asking for your growth. You may have been afraid to oblige because you've been afraid of growing. You're afraid to transform. Growth and transformation are beautiful. When you embrace this truth, life opens up to you in new and exciting ways.

Embrace Growth Opportunities

When life presents you with an opportunity to grow, don't just walk into it—run into it. Embrace your growth opportunities with both hands. A seed planted in the name of growth is never a dud. There is always a harvest. Earlier I said that growth comes before transformation. The more you are willing to grow, the more you will experience your life transform.

What's a growth opportunity?

- Anything that looks like a failure (divorce, being fired, arrested, etc.)
- Anything that makes you doubt your abilities or worth
- Anything you do not currently know
- Anything that challenges the status quo
- Anything that breaks your heart
- Criticism

🦋 Anything that requires you to give up the good to go for the great

Go Past Your Usual Stopping Point

Stretch yourself to go past the point where you usually stop. Maybe that spot is too risky for you to cross. Perhaps the timing has always been wrong or the investment too costly. It could be that you've been too winded to travel another step. Venture past those points.

You don't have to zoom past it. Just go a little further than you usually go. Each time you push past the spot where you'd normally stop, if even just a millimeter further, you reset the goalpost. Reset the goalpost over and over again, and the sky will become the limit. You can literally achieve anything.

Grow into the Person You Need to Be for the Next Season of Your Life

Every season of your life requires a new version of yourself. Instinctively we know this to be true during certain seasons of transformation. If you're bringing new life into the world, you know that in some aspects you too have to grow.

I'm single. I've lived on my own and provided for myself for years. I do what I want, when I want, and how I want. I have aspirations of being a wife and mother one day. I am fully aware that single Charlene cannot stay in married Charlene's house, at least not for long. If she does, it won't end well.

You Are Meant to Transform

People who are creating lives they love cannot be the versions of themselves who settle for whatever life throws their way.

A single person has to grow into a married person. A corporate worker has to grow into an entrepreneur. A subordinate has to grow into the leader. A person who lacks confidence yet has big, hairy, audacious goals has to grow into a confident person.

People often say they don't feel as though they are good enough to pursue their goals. I tend to agree. You may not be good enough for what you want to create in your future *right now*. That's why you have to grow into the person who is well able to create the vision.

If you can accept that the future you requires the current you to grow, you will never be limited by who you are today.

Getting Real

What do you need to shed to create a life you love?

_____
_____
_____

What promptings do you feel in your spirit?

_____
_____
_____

What growth opportunities are you ready to embrace?

_____
_____
_____

3 The Truth about Purpose

Purpose and transformation go hand in hand. Your purpose will require your transformation, and your transformation will lead you to your purpose. Furthermore, if you really want to create a life you love, you have to be on purpose. Doing what you know you are meant to do and doing it well brings unsurpassed satisfaction.

I often talk to women who say that they don't know what their purpose is and they want to find it. Everyone's looking for their purpose. And for good reason. It gives life meaning.

I ask these women, "What do you think it is? What do you think your purpose is?"

They all say some variation of "I think it is" some particular thing, "but…"

One woman said to me, "I think it is teaching. I've always wanted to be a teacher. I've always loved education, and I've always loved kids, but I just can't pass this certification test."

Another woman answered, "I think it's nursing. I've always wanted to be a nurse, but I just can't afford to go back to school."

There's always a "I think…but…"

I want to help you get rid of the "but" behind your purpose by sharing with you some simple truths about your purpose.

It Wants You as Much as You Want It

Your purpose is not hiding from you. It's not playing hide-and-seek. It's not trying to confuse you or trip you up in any way. Your purpose wants you just as much as you want it.

When we're asking the question "What is my purpose?" we're not asking the right question.

Many women have said to me, "I don't know what my purpose is."

Yet when I ask them, "What do you think it is?" I've never had anyone say, "I don't know. I have no idea."

There's always an idea, because your purpose is always talking to you. All the inspirations, all the ideas, all the instances of "that would be nice" or "that seems interesting" are a part of the path to your purpose. All these promptings on you are something wanting to connect with you and speak to you. It's not hiding itself from you. You're just not listening.

The Truth About Purpose

Growing up, I loved to write. When I wasn't at school, you could often find me sitting in my room writing. I wrote poems and songs for fun. My school writings were often recognized in school publications and contests.

In high school I was in the gifted program. As a part of the program, we had to take on a project. My project was writing a book.

Mr. Jones, my math teacher, asked me during class what my project would be.

"I am writing a book!" I said.

Joannie, seated behind me, smacked her teeth.

"Don't smack your teeth at me!" I snapped.

Clearly she was hating on my vision. I didn't end up writing a full-fledged book. Instead, I wrote a collection of poetry. Writing a book was a significant endeavor for a sixteen-year-old.

The idea to write a book wasn't planted in my heart yesterday or yesteryear. This vision has been building for more than fifteen years. Even when I forgot all about it, it stayed tucked inside my heart for just the right moment. This isn't even the first book I've sat down to write.

Writing a book has been a part of my purpose for many years. There have been false starts. There have been seasons of forgetfulness on my part. Yet the purpose has been unwavering.

Sometimes those things that come up for you over and over again are a clue to your purpose. What keeps coming up for you?

Another clue is your feelings about the world around you. For example, some things you feel pulled toward. Some things light you up. Some things you love to do and be a part of. Some things inspire and excite you. What are those things?

There are other things that you are drawn away from. There is a feeling of "Get me away from here. This doesn't feel right. I don't like it. I don't fit in."

Acknowledging how you respond and interact with your world is key to understanding your purpose. Things that excite or trigger you are often attached to your purpose.

Your purpose is always communicating with you through your interests, your personality, and your reactions to the world around you. Remember, it's not a secret. I've never had anyone say, "I haven't the slightest idea what my purpose is" because it's not a secret.

It's Bigger Than Vocation

The main message of this book is that the purpose of life is to grow. Whenever you are growing and stretching yourself, you are on purpose. However true that statement is, I realize that's a blanket purpose. It applies to all humanity. You're looking for what you specifically should be doing with your life.

When I think about my own purpose, I don't think my purpose is to be a coach or investor. I don't think my purpose is to write this book. Sure, those are things I am purposed to do, but they are not my purpose.

Purpose is bigger than vocation. It is bigger than any actions or accomplishments we can perform. Purpose is a state of being. It's a way of living. It's not always what you do. It is what you bring to what you do.

Purpose is listening to your own soul and paying attention to your own interests and consistently following that direction. It is following your own curiosities. Your purpose is found as you habitually act in accordance to the internal promptings that tug at your heart.

It's Not a Fairy Tale

We have this idea that our purpose is supposed to go smoothly. We think it's like walking in a crowded room, and as we walk through the door, everyone to the left and to the right steps back and makes a walkway for us. We think that our purpose is making a walkway for us. It's going to be smooth and easy sailing, but that's simply not true.

Your purpose will pull you, and sometimes it will drag you. Your purpose will leave you bloody and bruised and discouraged at times, and you won't want to keep going. Many a times, I've found myself asking, "Charlene, why are you doing this? Won't you stop it? Why don't you go spend your money on something else? Go buy a pair of shoes or something."

Whether it's investing in real estate, my personal development, or writing and publishing this book, I've invested tens of thousands of dollars many times over. I try to convince myself just to leave well enough alone. I've always had a good life with above-average income. I've always lived well enough. I could just relax and not rock the boat. Yet I can't just leave well enough alone. There's always a pull for something more.

When I first started in real-estate investing, I had a hard time finding a property. In hindsight it wasn't that hard, but at the time, it felt like it. When you're buying real estate for the purpose of investing and building wealth, you want to purchase a property that is a deal. It has to cost less than the current market value. Or the rent rate has to be greater than the mortgage payment. Otherwise it's not an investment. It's just buying a house.

I was working with a realtor at the time, and he would send me to look at houses that were not good deals. These houses had been on the market for over a year, and they were on par with market value.

I was thinking, "Dude, I want the same deals that everyone else wants. I don't want the deals that every other investor in this city has passed up on for a year."

It felt so hopeless. I thought to myself, "Just wait. Save some more money. Get a bigger down payment. The time is not right. Just wait."

That was what my mind was telling me to do—just wait. But my fingers kept dialing phone numbers. They kept dialing the numbers of people who could sell me a house and people who could help me buy a house.

I tried to convince myself, "Just wait. Stop. Just save your money. Give it a year." But I couldn't stop. I didn't stop.

That was my purpose calling me even when the humanness of who I was said, "The timing just isn't right."

Your purpose wants you as much as you want it. And it calls you even when you want to give up. Even when you're questioning why you're doing it and why you keep investing money and time, your purpose keeps calling you.

The pieces didn't just fall into place for me. And my second investment house was horrible. Everything that could go wrong did go wrong. If my first house was equivalent to walking into a crowded room with no walkway, my second house was me standing outside drenched in a brutal thunderstorm banging on the door begging to come in.

Getting to your purpose is not necessarily easy. There is no walkway. There are setbacks and heartbreaks. That's why we doubt if it's our purpose. The door isn't opening right away so it must be the wrong door. Sometimes that is true. Sometimes it's not true.

Jack Canfield said his mega hit *Chicken Soup for the Soul* was rejected 144 times[5], before someone decided to take on the project. There was no walkway for him. If he had decided this book was a mistake because the door didn't fling open upon his arrival, he wouldn't be the success he is today. He wouldn't have touched millions of lives.

Sergio Garcia won the 2017 Masters Golf Tournament. It took him nearly twenty years and seventy-three tries.[6] Yet eventually he won. If he had quit after year five or ten or even eighteen, he wouldn't have earned the privilege and honor to be clothed in the infamous green Masters jacket so few have worn.

There's More Than One

I just talked about real estate investing, and I talked about my love for personal growth and development. You don't have just one purpose. A lot of times, people think that it has to be this or that. "Either

---

[5] "Jack Canfield." In Super Soul Sunday. OWN. December 13, 15.
[6] MacLeary, John. "Sergio Garcia ends 18-year wait to win a major after 73 attempts - and sport's other broken hoodoos." The Telegraph. April 10, 2017. Accessed May 30, 2017. http://www.telegraph.co.uk/sport/2017/04/10/sergio-garcia-ends-18-year-wait-win-major-73-attempts-sports.

I'm a mom or a businesswoman" But you can have more than one purpose, and your purpose actually evolves. It's not even that you have one purpose throughout your lifetime. You could, but it's also likely that you have an evolution of a purpose.

Let's look back to the caterpillar and butterfly. There's a purpose for every stage in that life cycle. The caterpillar has a specific purpose: to eat and grow. The cocoon has a purpose: to transform. And the butterfly has a specific purpose. The butterfly, once it breaks free of the cocoon, is purposed to fly and find a mate to start the cycle all over again.

You can have more than one purpose at any given time. You can be working toward multiple things at any given time. You can also see an evolution and a shift of your purpose in the various seasons of your life.

There Will Be Detours

Sometimes when there's a detour, we start to question our purpose. When a door is closed in our face or when something doesn't work out how we wanted it to work out, we question if this was in fact our purpose.

Sandy had a great job opportunity in another state and was really excited about it. She quit her job and canceled the lease on her apartment. Sandy packed up her things and moved to her new home state eager to begin the adventure awaiting her. She didn't know anyone in this new state. She moved there only for the promises of an exciting career expedition. Yet, once she got there, the job opportunity was no longer available.

She was crushed and discouraged. She doubted herself, believing that she made a mistake and took a wrong turn somewhere. Sandy thought that her purpose was in the job, but it may have just been in the state.

Your purpose wants you as much as you want it, so it's not going to leave you. You might leave it. You might not pursue it, but it's not going to leave you. Sometimes there are detours.

It's similar to meditation. When you first start meditating, you're often taught to use a mantra. A mantra is a statement that you repeat to yourself. The mantra is designed to help get you to meditation—to get you out of your thoughts and to the meditative state. Once you are there, you're supposed to drop the mantra. The mantra isn't supposed to be meditation. It's supposed to get you to the meditation.

Sometimes what we're experiencing in our life isn't supposed to be the purpose. It is simply supposed to get us there. Sandy leaving her job and taking on this new job wasn't the purpose. It was to get her to the purpose; she wouldn't have moved to that state, which was a critical part of her journey and her purpose, if it had not been for that job. But once she got there, she was able to drop the job. She dropped the mantra, so to speak. She didn't want to drop it, but it was dropped because it was no longer needed.

The detours are not a signal that you are on the wrong path. Sometimes it looks like you're headed in a certain direction because that's where you need to go for that leg of your journey. But when you're no longer needed on that particular road, you take a detour. Yet it's still in alignment with your purpose.

I know that sounds contradictory to the first truth. I said that I often ask women,

"What do you think your purpose is?" It's not a secret, so you have some inclination. Now I say the inclinations you have may not be your purpose. The ideas, beliefs, and knowledge that you have about your purpose now might not be the final destination, but they are critical to getting you to the final destination.

So even when you ask yourself, "Well, what do I think it is?" you could be wrong. But that insight and awareness is an important part of you getting to the destination.

Let Your Purpose SING

Strengths

Identifying your strengths is a good starting place when you want clarity on your purpose. Your strengths can be leveraged in the fulfillment of your purpose. What are you good at? What are you knowledgeable about? Who or what needs your strengths?

Not being strong in a certain area doesn't necessarily mean you're not meant for that area. It might just mean you need support. In the Bible, Moses wasn't a good speaker, so Aaron stepped in to be strong where Moses was weak. Together they fulfilled a purpose.

Interests

Your strengths alone aren't necessarily indicative of your purpose. You can have a job that you're really good at, yet every time you walk through the doors, a bit of your soul dies. Strengths plus interests can be a powerful purpose formula.

Your interests can point you toward your purpose. One of the reasons why I wrote this book is because I have a strong interest in personal growth and self-improvement. I've studied the field for years for fun, but in the process built strength. That combination has led me here. Follow (and strengthen) your interests, and find your purpose.

Needs

What does the world need? Or your neighborhood, city, state, etc.? The unresolved needs surrounding you can point you to the direction of your purpose for this season of your life. This is especially true if you have an intense passion or belief related to the need.

I know a man who walked from Atlanta to Washington, DC, to raise awareness of homelessness in the United States. He saw a need—homelessness. He had a belief—that everyone deserves a place to live. The blending of the need and the belief created a purpose.

Gifts

What are your innate gifts? This can be different from your strengths. Strengths can be created. Gifts cannot. By definition they are given to you free of charge. Gifts can and should be strengthened with practice, study, and training.

FROM CATERPILLAR TO BUTTERFLY

Beyoncé is gifted at singing. She has strengthened her gift likely with vocal coaching, practice, and study. I, on the other hand, cannot sing. No amount of coaching, practicing, or studying is going to make me a gifted singer.

What you were gifted with at birth is synced with your purpose.

    The other piece to all this is passion. If you are not passionate, it doesn't matter what your interests, gifts, or strengths are. The needs you see (if you can even see them) won't make a difference. Passion fuels purpose.
    I've worked with various people on my rental properties. They didn't always see what I saw. They couldn't see the small hole hiding beneath the windowsill or the wasps sliding in a crack in the fascia board likely returning to their nest. They didn't have my passion, so that didn't have my vision.
    Likewise, I've been in roles where I had no clue what to do. I wanted to add value. I wanted to give an honest day's work. I wanted to see the opportunity, but I couldn't. I needed my boss to direct my work. I was blinded by a lack of passion.
    Purpose without passion is dead. Passion creates vision. Vision leads to purpose.

The Question You Should Be Asking

The Truth About Purpose

When people say, "I want to know what my purpose is," it implies that they have a belief in God or a higher power. It implies that they believe that God has sent them to this earth for a specific purpose. They want to find it. If they do not believe that God gave them a purpose, then they wouldn't be asking, "What's my purpose?" They would just go and choose one. They would create their own purpose. But the fact that they're seeking a purpose means that they believe in God and that makes the first point even more so true. Because if God gave you the purpose, and it's a part of His plan, He wants you to know what it is. It's not a secret. When we're asking ourselves what's our purpose, we tend to be asking the wrong question. Because your purpose isn't hiding from you, "What's my purpose?" isn't the right question.

When we feel this hunger for our purpose, what we are really feeling is hunger for God because God has given you the purpose. That void that you feel in your life, the lack of direction, the unfulfillment, the dissatisfaction, is not a lack of purpose. It is a lack of connectedness to God, a lack of oneness to God. So the question is not "What is my purpose?"

The question is "How can I get closer to God, the giver of that purpose?" How can you enhance your spiritual practice to get closer to God? To have more of a oneness with God? That's really what you're seeking. That's what your hunger is about. It's about God. It's not about your "purpose."

Intimidated by Purpose

FROM CATERPILLAR TO BUTTERFLY

The alternative is that you are intimated by your purpose. You know very well what it is, but it scares the faith out of you. You know you would have to show up in the world a different way to truly fulfill your purpose. What it would require of you intimidates you. And that holds you back.

I've heard so many times that successful women intimidate men. That statement boils my blood.

"So what? Life is intimidating. Going on interviews is intimidating. Conducting a speech or presentation in a packed room is intimidating. Facing a trial or tribulation you don't have the skill, knowledge, or wherewithal to beat is intimidating. But such is life. Put your big-boy pants on and ask that woman out!" I passionately instruct.

And so I will tell you the same thing. So what if you're intimidated by your purpose. So what if you don't know what to do or how to get started. So what if you failed the test repeatedly. Put your big-girl pants on, and slay your purpose!

Getting Real

What do you think your purpose is?

_____
_____
_____

Is there anything that you can't let go of? The idea repeatedly comes up? You've been dreaming about it for years or even decades?

The Truth About Purpose

_____
_____
_____

What are your gifts?

_____
_____
_____

What is stopping you from claiming what you already know to be true about your purpose? What intimidates you about it? What are your doubts, insecurities, etc.?

_____
_____
_____

How can you get closer to God?

_____
_____
_____

Purpose Meditation

Take a deep breath in, and on the exhale, feel your body relax. Inhale once again. On the exhale, feel your body relax even more.

Imagine or pretend that your purpose is sitting next to you. And here is your opportunity to ask of it anything you'd like to know. Look over to your purpose and ask your purpose what it wants you to do next.

"Purpose, what would you have me do next?" Just listen. You're not listening from your thoughts or your brain or your mental space. You're listening from your heart, your soul, your intuition. If it helps, place both hands on your heart. And again, ask your purpose what it wants you to do next.

You can ask your purpose any other questions you want to know. You might ask your purpose, what is it that it wants you to know about it. "Purpose, what should I know about you and the role you want to play in my life?" Listen. Any other questions you have for your purpose, ask them. And then listen with your heart.

Count slowly to three. On three, return to complete awareness feeling more connected and more in tune with your purpose.

I encourage you to grab a pen and paper right now and jot down anything that came up for you during this meditation. If nothing came up for you, which is perfectly normal, that's okay. Continue this meditation over time. Make it a practice to be able to hear from your heart, to be able to hear from your spirit so that you can move forward in the direction that is best for you to move forward again.

Download free meditation audio at
fromcaterpillarstobutterflies.com/specialgift

4 Be Content Where You Are

"You're so miserable. You're so unhappy. You just hate life." I heard a coach say this once.

I thought, "I don't know who she is talking to, but she is not talking to me." I wondered, "Why are you inviting people to participate in a pity party parade?"

We wear our misery like a badge of honor. We wear dissatisfaction like a mark of distinction. "Look at me! Look at how miserable I am. Look at how dissatisfied I am."

I am not getting into agreement with any negative feelings or emotions about life. You shouldn't either.

Life is a series of journeys. We should always be working toward something. We should always be going somewhere, believing in something, or being pulled by some vision. We should always be putting our energy, effort, and love toward the realization of a goal or vision. Progress is a huge part of life.

When we don't have anything to work toward or believe in, it kills us. Sometimes it physically kills us. There have been many stories of the ambitious fifty-year career veteran who retires from his or her passion and then shortly thereafter dies. Not having purpose kills us. It kills us spiritually, emotionally, and mentally. If we're not believing in something, if we're not on some type of journey that empowers us, then we're as good as dead.

Life is a series of journeys of setting goals and accomplishing goals, of seeing a vision and walking toward that vision, of believing in something and going to get it. If you can accept this as true, and you're miserable every time you're in the gap between where you are and where you want to be, you're going to spend a lifetime being miserable. You're going to spend a lifetime being unhappy. You're going to spend a lifetime being dissatisfied. If you don't learn how to be satisfied and content in the gap, you're in for a lifetime of misery. There's always a gap. You can have a vision for something more without despising where you are. You can choose to focus on the satisfying parts of life.

We've been trained to focus on those things we find dissatisfying. Our default is to zoom in closely on the bad things in life. Bad news travels fast, as they say. I challenge you to shift focus to the things you find satisfying.

A guy went around asking unsuspecting people, "What do you most want out of life?"

Be Content Where You Are

Every single person said some variation of, "I want to be happy."

If you feel the same—you just want to be happy—you cannot be miserable. You cannot be in despair. You've got to be happy. This requires that you focus on what you're satisfied with and not what you're dissatisfied with.

A law of attraction teacher once said, "Your momentum toward achieving what you desire increases in satisfaction."

When you want something for yourself, you can't be miserable. You can't despise where you are while you're on the way to where you want to be next. Why? Because when you're in despair, you're not going to have the energy, the hope, or the motivation to get up off the couch to work on what you want next. When you're in despair, it is soul-crushing. It kills your motivation. It kills your desire.

Your momentum toward achieving what you desire increases in satisfaction because satisfaction helps you focus. Despair takes you off track. When you are in despair, you just want to reach for the quickest thing that will bring pleasure.

I've had horrible days at work. I've had seasons where I hated my job, but I had to go in anyway. I'd go to work and be so dissatisfied for eight hours straight. I wasn't leveraging my strengths. I was bored and unchallenged. I hated it. And then I'd go home and run to the fridge, thinking, "What can I eat?"

Why? Because eating something yummy is satisfying. It is satisfying enough to kill the despair for a moment. But then I'd have to start all over again the next day.

Being in despair doesn't help you. It doesn't help you create momentum. It doesn't help you be happy. It doesn't help you close the gap. Being satisfied and learning to be content helps you do those things. It is in your best interest to focus on the satisfying parts of life.

I believe life is like a yin-yang symbol. The yin-yang symbol is a circle. One half is black, and the other is white. There's a black dot in the white half, and there's a white dot in the black half. The yin-yang symbol says that there's good inside of evil and evil inside of good. There's life inside of death and death inside of life.

What I've learned is that there is dissatisfaction inside of satisfaction and satisfaction inside of dissatisfaction. If you want to be happy and enjoy your life that is a series of journeys, then you have to focus on the satisfaction that is always there. That's the yin and yang of life. Focus on the satisfying parts.

My sister graduated from college with her PhD. The weekend of the graduation, a lot of family came in from out of town. We had a big party and barbecue at my mom's house. My dad came into town from Kentucky. My dad and my grandma stayed at my sister's house, which is a good bit away from the party.

At the party everyone was having a good time. We were barbecuing. We were socializing. We were joking and laughing. My cousin was on the ones and twos (in other words he was the DJ). In the midst of all the festivities, my dad walked up to me and said they were ready to go back to my sister's house. They had a car, but he wanted me to go too so they could follow behind me.

"Ugh!" I thought, refraining from rolling my eyes and showing how irritated I was. I was annoyed! We hadn't even cut the cake yet. I was having fun. It was going to take me an hour to go to my sister's house and come back.

Then I thought, "Okay, Charlene, is this dissatisfaction inside of satisfaction?"

Because the truth of the matter was that it was. It was a very satisfying weekend. It was a very satisfying party. Having to leave the party for an hour was a bout of dissatisfaction. Such is life.

I could have said, "No, I'm not going to lead you to Marlene's house. Use your GPS."

But why? He was my father. Leaving him to get back to my sister's house alone would have made the dissatisfaction intensify. An argument could have ensued. Feelings could have been hurt. Plus my father was worth my inconvenience, and I didn't want to be disrespectful to my parents.

Since it was dissatisfaction inside of satisfaction, I decided to just let it go. I decided to focus on the satisfying aspects of the weekend. Again, there is always something satisfying to focus on.

If you train yourself to focus on what's satisfying, you will improve your relationships. How many times have you nitpicked your spouse or friend over something that was trivial? It was not even a deal breaker, and you were picking a fight over it. When you shift your thoughts to what's satisfying, you'll see relationships improve. In fact, your overall experience of life will improve.

Sometimes we want to focus on what's dissatisfying because we think that our attention makes it better. If we ignore it, it will only get worse. So we tell everybody every time we're dissatisfied.

I was next in line at the checkout counter. Two other patrons filed in behind me. There were two cashiers and one line. A woman approached the line and loudly said to her son, "We're going to go to this cashier." They promptly went to stand behind the customer being served at the register furthest away.

A more courteous person would have understood that there was one line for the next available cashier. Yet she bypassed the line, rationalizing it by suggesting that the three customers in line were committed to only being served by the one cashier.

There's an older version of Charlene who would have told her about herself; however, I did not. I didn't say a thing, and neither did the two men behind me. It wasn't worth a confrontation.

However, I did want her to know I disapproved. I gave her the evil eye. My doing so added no value to either of our lives. She probably didn't even notice.

It's the same thing with your dissatisfaction. You think that if you just ignore it or focus on the satisfying part, then what you're basically doing is condoning it. You have to let it be known that you're not satisfied. You think you're settling or accepting it because you are choosing to shift your focus away from it. But you're not.

Yes, you are focusing on the satisfying parts as a way of life, but you're also going to acknowledge what's dissatisfying. They key is not to dwell on the dissatisfaction. Dwelling on dissatisfaction steal happiness which is counterproductive to creating the life you love. Adopt the mantra "Acknowledge, but don't dwell."

Being in a situation that is not satisfying to you is not a curse. Actually it's a blessing. There is a pretty good chance that the situation you find yourself in right now that is dissatisfying was once satisfying. Over time that satisfaction has shifted. You've grown. You've been exposed to new things. You have enhanced your skill set. What used to be satisfying is no longer satisfying. That's life.

The friction that you feel now is just your cue. It's your indication that it's time for you to start another journey. It's the same friction that the caterpillar feels that makes it build a cocoon. It's the same friction that birds and mammals feel when it's time to migrate. It's the friction the seed feels when it's ready to sprout into a plant and break ground.

The friction is just your indication that you have stayed on this journey long enough and it's time to start a new journey. It's not a curse.

When you find yourself in a dissatisfying situation, you want first to identify if you are experiencing satisfaction inside of dissatisfaction or dissatisfaction inside of satisfaction. If it's dissatisfaction inside of satisfaction, then decide just to let it go. However, if it is satisfaction inside of dissatisfaction, you should make a change.

When it's satisfaction inside of dissatisfaction, the first thing you should keep in mind is that it's critical to maintain your focus on the satisfying parts. Dwelling on the dissatisfaction will stall your progress.

Next, get crystal clear on what's dissatisfying. If it's your job, what's dissatisfying about it? Is it your coworkers? Is it the work that you're doing? Do you not feel challenged? Do you not feel any passion?

FROM CATERPILLAR TO BUTTERFLY

This is a really important step. If you're not clear enough, then you might go solve the wrong problem. You might go from the frying pan to the fire. Get clarity on what you dislike so you can address the right problem.

Once you're clear on what you don't want, get super clear on what you'd most prefer. Where would you most rather be?

Once you've identified that gap between where you are and where you want to be, it's time to identify how you're going to close it.

Closing the gap is the journey that I said we're always on. Identifying the gap is not a journey. Identifying a gap is standing still. If you've identified a gap but haven't started walking the journey, this might be what's causing you some despair.

Find out how to close the gap. What do you need? Who do you need to know? Where do you need to go?

To summarize, know where you are and why you don't want to be there. Know where you'd most rather be, and know what you need to get there. At the very least, know where you're interested in possibly being.

A lot of women I coach say they don't know where they want to be. This not knowing keeps them stuck; however, you do not have to know exactly where you want to go. You just have to know what interests you and explore those interests. Simply be interested in finding out if you're interested.

Start taking action to close the gap or even exploring your interests. If you're in action, there's no reason to walk around pitiful or in despair.

Imagine being told you're two months pregnant and then being miserable because the baby is not here. Well, it needs time. So when you've identified where you're going and you start going, there's no reason for you to be unhappy. There's no reason for you to be dissatisfied. You are working on it. Give yourself some credit. Be patient with yourself.

But in the meantime, focus on what you are satisfied with because there's always satisfaction somewhere that you could be focused on. As long as you are on the journey and committed to the journey, you're going to get there. And if you're going to get there in due time, there's no reason to be dissatisfied.

If I give you turn-by-turn directions from your house to my house and you follow the directions, you will get to my house. It's just what it is. You might have to do some course corrections. There might be some road closures or weather problems. You might have to change things up, but you will get here if you follow the directions. And you will not be in your car cursing life because you are not here. You will know that you're on your way. You can just sit back and enjoy the journey.

Sit back and enjoy all the journeys you find yourself on. Be satisfied in the midst.

Avoid This Pitfall

Sometimes when we find ourselves in a dissatisfying situation, we catch a small glimmer of satisfaction that causes us to stumble. I was in a dissatisfying relationship with Marcus for years. So many times I was ready to leave. "It's over this time for real!" I'd commit.

And then Marcus would do something nice and thoughtful. "Okay. Well, this is satisfying. It's not so bad. He's trying. Maybe I should stay." Inevitably I'd be back to being dissatisfied again.

Be mindful that there is satisfaction inside of dissatisfaction, but overarching, what is the situation? What is the relationship? What is the career? If it's mostly dissatisfaction, focus on the satisfying parts of that so that you're not miserable, but don't let the satisfaction distract you. You'll lose the momentum that you're creating. Be committed to changing your situation without letting the small moments of satisfaction make you get comfortable or confused.

Practice Gratitude

A consistent practice of gratitude can help you be content where you are. Here are two methods I personally use to practice gratitude.

Gratitude Journal

A gratitude journal is a journal specifically for capturing what you are grateful for. You can use a regular notebook found at any retail or grocery store. Alternatively you can purchase a gratitude journal if you prefer.

Each night jot down a few things you're thankful for. It doesn't have to be anything miraculous. Sometimes I'm just thankful for my bed. I am thankful for my dog or that I had a meal that day. I'm thankful for my family.

It is really the small things that show up on my gratitude list. I don't have humongous things I'm grateful for every day.

That's the beauty of it. You can find something to be grateful for every single day if you look out for it.

A lot of times we are waiting for something miraculous to happen in our lives before we get thankful, but it's really the day-to-day things. Sometimes we neglect to appreciate the ordinariness of life. Don't think that life is supposed to be spectacular every day, with fireworks every night. It's the ordinary experiences of life that we can be most grateful for.

Blessing or Gratitude Jar

This is similar to the gratitude journal. I have a blessing jar in my kitchen. Every time I experience a blessing, I cut a stripe from an index card and write it down. Here are some of my real-life examples:

- Approved for Haiti missions trip; 4/27.
- Best speaker third time in a row; 6/14 (at Toastmasters).
- Asked for discount and received a free ticket; 3/10 (to a conference).
- Spending New Year's Day with family making blessing jars; 1/1.
- Losing inches! Before and after pics look good; 2/28.

Nothing earth-shattering, but nonetheless everyday things to be grateful for.

When you are content and grateful in your current season, you accomplish two things. First you position yourself to enjoy every day of your life. That's what we all want—to be happy every single day of our lives. Second you create the right atmosphere for you to achieve your desires in the next season.

FROM CATERPILLAR TO BUTTERFLY

Being content is a powerful tool to help you transform your life. And it sets the right foundation for the other tools you'll learn throughout this book to be applied. Beyond being a powerful tool, being content is a powerful way of life.

Getting Real

Is this current season of your life satisfaction inside of dissatisfaction or the opposite?

_____
_____
_____

What are your next steps based on your previous answer? (You will either let it go or close the gap. How?)

_____
_____
_____

What are you grateful for?

1.

2.

3.

4.

5 Change Your Frequency to Change Your Life

You can change your life by changing your frequency to a higher vibration.

You may be thinking, "How can I change my frequency to change my life if I don't even know what it means?" At least that was what I thought the first half-dozen times I heard the word.

In its simplest form and the context of this book, the frequency from which you operate your life is a representation of your recurring thoughts, attitudes, perspectives, and beliefs. From here come your decisions, actions, and behaviors. Your decisions, actions, and behaviors then set the direction for your life.

When you change your frequency, the wave of energy that initiates the ripple effect leading to your life's gradual unfoldment, you can change your life.

Spiritual teacher Mary Morrissey told this story at her popular three-day live event.[7] As a young wife and mother, she convinced her husband to accompany her to a personal growth seminar.

During the seminar, the teacher said to the class, "Nothing bad ever happens to you in life." The teacher advised, "When something 'bad' happens to you, don't think of it as being bad." Instead of reacting and zeroing in on how bad this thing is, "give yourself three days before you react. Don't have an opinion about it for three full days. In the process of those three days, ask yourself what good could come from this."

If nothing bad ever happens to you, surely something good has to come from all of life's so-called misfortunes.

Mary was studying at a university at the time while her husband worked outside the home. One day her husband arrived home from work. He was clearly bothered and in a funk.

Mary asked, "What's wrong?"

He proceeded to tell her that he and several other people were let go from their jobs that day.

Of course she wanted to freak out. She was a young mother. She didn't have a job. Her husband, the sole provider, had just lost his source of income.

Her husband said, "Well, let's follow the teacher's advice. Let's wait three days and see how it goes. While we're waiting,

---

[7] Mary Morrissey, "DreamBuilder Live" (seminar, Westin Dallas Park Central, Dallas, TX, October 21, 2016).

let's think of ways that we can make this turn out for our good."

The two sat down to write a list of what good could come from the layoff. Here's what the list read:

- ❦ The ninety-minute commute to work could be drastically reduced.
- ❦ Husband could find a job that paid him more money.
- ❦ He could find a job that required him to work fewer hours.

Ultimately the husband got a new job that was closer to their home, paid him more money, and required him to work fewer hours.

This is where frequency comes in. I finally understood when I heard this story. If a young Mary and her husband had not gone to that event, they might have followed their first impulse, which would have been to freak out. They would have likely panicked. Panic is a frequency that creates an adverse set of outcomes because the ideas, solutions, and next steps that are generated when you are freaking out are different than what you would create when you are calm and focused on what you really want.

Defensive versus Offensive Frequency

There are two main types of frequency: the defensive frequency and the offensive frequency. The defensive frequency asks, "How do I stop the bottom from falling out?"

How do I stop this from getting any worse? How do I just maintain what I have?

The offensive frequency asks, "What do I really want, and what's going to get me there?"

If the couple were panicking, their list of next steps might have read like this:

- Mary drops out of school.
- Mary gets a job.
- Sell the family house and car.

This is a very different list from the previous one. The ideas and the next steps that derive from the defensive frequency are geared toward keeping the bottom from falling out.

The ramifications for this frequency are long term and wide. How many people do you know who have taken an action that was meant to be temporary just to stop the bleeding, and then it became permanent?

You may have temporarily put a goal on the back burner, and years later it is still there. I talk to women all the time who say they haven't dreamed in years. One woman told me she hadn't dreamed since her daughter was born.

"How old is your daughter?" I asked.

"Thirteen years old."

Imagine not having a dream in your heart for thirteen long years. Major life events such as motherhood, marriage, or divorce can shift your frequency to a lower vibration. Be careful of this.

When you're on an offensive frequency, you're always thinking about what you're grateful for and what you most want out of life. You are focused on the actions you need to take to get you there. Being offensive means not being taken off track when an unexpected event or setback comes up. When you're offensive, there are no other tracks to take. You never take your dreams off the table.

Always focus on how to score the next point in the game of life. Ask yourself:

- "What good could come out of this?"

Change Your Frequency to Change Your Life

- ✺ "How do I make this situation in alignment with my vision?"
- ✺ "What am I most thankful for right now?"

Being offensive means not allowing temporary situations to drive you to make permanent or long-lasting decisions. It means not ignoring all the good in your life while dwelling on all the "bad."

Take the woman who has a vision to get her degree and teach; if she drops out of school at a defensive frequency, she is not moving in the direction of her vision. She's not playing the game of life on the offensive team. Maybe money is tight. But money being tight is a temporary situation.

Your frequency is either the offensive frequency or the defensive frequency. You can't be both at the same time. The offensive frequency is going to move you toward your highest vision for your life.

The defensive frequency is what is going to stop you from sinking any lower than where you are right now. It's about maintenance. It's not about growth.

Are you living your life from the growth, offensive frequency or a maintenance, defensive frequency? It's the difference between maintaining the life you have and growing it into a more beautiful, fulfilling life.

Hopefully you can see how the person who is freaking out isn't creating his or her best life. The person who is focused on maintenance and defense is not creating the best life either because that person is not focusing on the vision.

Those who are focused on offensive play and growth are the ones who are creating the lives that they really want. They're not settling for the life that they don't want, and they're not focused on what they don't want. They're keeping their focus on where they really want to go and what they most want out of life while maintaining an attitude of gratitude.

You change your frequency by changing your thoughts. By changing your thoughts and reactions, you're making sure that your actions lead you to where you most want to go. Thoughts become things because your thoughts become your actions. You have to make sure that your thoughts are aligned with where you want to go. Pay no mind to where you don't want to go. That is how you transform your life.

Declutter

The first thing that people can do to shift their frequency is declutter their space.

I moved into my house seven years ago. There are some things that went from the moving truck to the garage, and they have stayed there for seven years. Every time I got in my car, I saw the boxes and thought, "I should really get those up. I've got to do something with them. I don't know how to clean this mess up. I don't have the time to clean this mess up." At least twice a day on most days, I am in the garage. I'm walking to my car or from the car to my house.

In that moment when I'm thinking, "I've got to clean this mess up," I'm not thinking from a place of gratitude. I'm not thinking, "I love this stuff. I love my space." I'm not thinking, "I'm so thankful to have this." I'm thinking, "I've got to get rid of it. I don't like it. It's a mess. It's too much." Those seconds that I'm thinking about that, and even minutes if I dwell on it, they add up to hours over time. All the hours of my life that I spent thinking about the things that I don't want or like are taking me off the frequency that I need to be on to create what I really want to create.

If I'm thinking about what I don't want in my garage, I have occupied space that could have been better served thinking about what I really do want in my life. Decluttering your space can help you shift your frequency for this reason.

Declutter everything. Declutter your house, your car, and your garage. You even want to declutter your purse and your desk. Every time you look at clutter in your space, there's a possibility that it is going to trigger your frequency to defense. You'll be focused on what you don't want or what you don't have. By immediately removing the stimuli, the things that stimulate your defensive thinking, you will be more likely to focus your thinking on offensive, high-frequency thoughts rather than low-frequency thoughts.

Start with the things that are the most distracting for you. Don't go to your junk drawer because you probably don't go into your junk drawer every day. If you're like me, you do walk through your garage every day. The garage would be a better place to start. Whatever your particular situation, start with the things that are most taxing for you. Whatever keeps you on the lower frequency the most often and serves you the least should get your attention first. Then keep going until everything is decluttered.

Give yourself some rules around decluttering. This is what happens oftentimes. You say, "Well, I'm going to sell this on e-Bay," or "I'm going to have a yard sale," or "I'm going to give this to such and such." Then you don't do it. The clutter stays.

As you are decluttering your house and deciding what you're going to do with your items, you need to give yourself a deadline. If you're going to sell something online, you need to post it online within a certain time frame. If it's not done, then it gets donated or goes into the trash can. If it doesn't sell within a certain time frame, then it gets donated. It doesn't get to be listed somewhere for two years so that it can just stay in your house. Give yourself some rules. Have an accountability partner to help you if you need support in following through.

Go through your house, and decide what stays, what goes, and by what time line it goes. If it doesn't go by that time line, either by selling it or by giving it to someone else, then it has to be donated or thrown away. Don't let this linger forever.

I learned this next tip at a Jack Canfield seminar.[8] He says that you should go to your house and fix or remove everything that you don't feel good about. It's not necessarily clutter, but it is broken or you don't like it. Again, when you walk past something in your house that's broken—it could be a broken clock or appliance—it has the ability to trigger low-frequency thoughts.

In my master bathroom, I have his-and-her sinks. I dropped something down the drain in one of the sinks. I needed it back! I took the pipe off the sink and retrieved my belonging, but I couldn't get the pipe back on. I stopped using that sink. It wasn't

---

[8] Jack Canfield, "One Day to Greatness" (seminar, Hyatt Regency Dallas Hotel, Dallas, TX, November 5, 2016).

usable unless I wanted to ruin the cabinet beneath it. That broken sink shifted my thoughts to what I didn't want, what needed to change, and what I was not thankful for. I was thinking I really had to get that fixed. I wondered how much a plumber would cost. I had so much to do. I didn't have time. I'd rather spend my money on something else. I was spinning my thoughts on a low-frequency area.

To limit low-frequency thoughts, go through your house and fix the things that are broken. Even if it's not broken, but you just don't like something, get rid of it. It could be as simple as not liking the color of a wall. Fix what's broken or undesired so that you can stop triggering your thoughts to focus on low-frequency things.

Address and Avoid

Everyone says that they want to have lives of happiness, peace of mind, joy, and fulfillment. We profess to want a life of purpose and meaning, but we are busy distracting ourselves with insignificant matters. Namely, we entertain drama.

Drama is a low-frequency activity, and it is a distraction. It is a distraction from what you are really feeling. It is the avoidance of sitting with yourself in your mess, feelings, insecurities, jealousies, or hurts. It is the avoidance of acknowledging it so that you can process it and grow through it.

You cannot raise your frequency if you refuse to acknowledge it is on a low vibration. The avoidance that drama allows you to experience is counterproductive to creating the life you want. If you can't sit in your mess, how can you clean it up? If you can't process how you feel, then you can't address it. If you can't process how the life around you is unfolding, then you can't be a participant in how that life around you unfolds.

People think that drama is their friend because it keeps from feeling what they are truly feeling. Some people are addicted to it. They are addicted to drama because they are addicted to not feeling.

Drama is unconstructive behavior and communication. Having a conversation with someone in a constructive way is not drama. It is the constructive communication and behavior that is helping you grow, resolve, and move forward. When you're in the midst of drama, you are in the midst of unconstructive behavior and communication.

Drama is gossip, slander, intentional disrespect, name calling, initiating arguments, sharing negative opinions about others, and other pointless communication. It's often used to agitate or get a response out of someone.

Drama can also be making a scene or causing an issue when it is just as easy to do the opposite. For example, Mary used to call her son Rob's home. If Rob's wife answered the phone, Mary would hang up without saying anything. She wanted to make a point that she didn't like Rob's wife. That's drama.

When you find yourself in the middle of drama, it is because you have created it or you have decided to participate in it. Either you are the person who is creating the drama or you are participating in drama that other people bring to you. Either way it's not good, and you have to learn to cut it out of your life.

If you've created drama, then you can equally stop it. If you don't want to stop the drama or find it challenging, then you need to pay attention to where that's coming from. Why are you feeding off this? What is it that you really don't want to acknowledge about yourself and what you are really feeling?

If someone else is bringing you drama, learn to respond, "Thank you, but I'm not interested."

This doesn't mean that if something is happening you can't address it. It means that you're going to address it constructively. You're not going to get caught up in the emotion and the heat of the destructive behavior.

Instead you're going to put yourself in the driver's seat. You're not just going along for the ride anymore because that's what happens when someone brings you drama. They're running the show. You have just agreed to go along for the ride. There are implications to your life for doing that.

Some people will create drama in your life because they are distracting themselves from something. They have feelings of jealousy or inferiority that they are trying to suppress. Maybe they are insecure or simply bored. Be mindful of these people because you'll be wreaking havoc in your life due to someone else's avoidance.

When you find yourself in drama, acknowledge, "This is a distraction. Who is trying to be distracted? Is it me, or is it them?"

If it's them, why do you care? You should have the attitude, "I'm not going to ruin my life because you are trying to distract yourself."

And if that's you, you should resolve not to operate on a low frequency. Don't let gossip; he said, she said; or any other drama keep you from your best life. When you address the real issue and avoid the drama, you put yourself in the driver's seat.

Don't participate in the drama. Stay focused on the real issue. Reflect on it, sit with it, and address it if it needs to be addressed from a constructive point of view. If it's not worth addressing, move on.

Pause

The third thing you can do to change your frequency borrows from the advice of the personal growth teacher I mentioned earlier. You're simply going to pause. When you find yourself facing minor inconveniences or triggers, pause and wait thirty minutes before you react.

I attended a seminar hosted by a popular bestselling author. Once it was over, there was a book signing, and the line grew long fast. I was starting to get irritated. But then I said to myself, "Okay, I'm going to give myself thirty minutes before I allow myself to get irritated. I'm just going to be cool and mellow for thirty minutes."

By the time the thirty minutes came, the line had moved. I was out of that place in thirty minutes. With minor inconveniences such as getting stuck in traffic, your child bringing an F home on the report card, or the line at the grocery store, give yourself thirty minutes before you react. Don't judge the situation or decide that it's bad for thirty minutes.

For bigger inconveniences or issues like getting fired or ending a relationship, give yourself three days before you react, before you decide that this is bad for you and freaking out. In the process of those three days, reflect on what good could come from this.

See

The last step is to spend time focusing on what you really want. That means spending time daydreaming and visioning what you want for your future. This should be uninterrupted thought time. Allow your thoughts and desires to flow freely. Don't stop a thought or limit a desire because you think it's unattainable. Instead you are really allowing yourself to go there, to go far and deep into your vision for life. You're not rebutting anything. You're not debating with yourself. You're not giving yourself any reason why you cannot do it. You're just going to give yourself uninterrupted time of at least ten minutes a day. Make visualizing what you most want to have out of life a daily practice.

Ask yourself, "What do I really want to achieve? What is most appealing to me in my future?"

Focus on your vision as often as possible. We'll talk more about vision in the next chapter.

Getting Real

What low-frequency triggers show up in your life?

_____
_____
_____

Is there drama that you create or participate in? If so, what is it distracting you from?

_____
_____
_____

What's your biggest vision for your future?

_____
_____
_____

6 Expand Your Vision to Expand Your Life

The Bible says that you have not because you ask not. I believe that you ask not because you see not. You cannot achieve what you cannot see. Everything is created twice. It is created once in your mind and then once in reality. You cannot create in the physical what you cannot conceive in your mind.

If your life is uninspiring, if it hasn't taken you where you wanted to be at this point, it is probably because you have had a limited vision. This chapter will teach you how you can expand that vision and then watch your life follow.

Oprah Winfrey is quoted as saying, "Create the highest, grandest vision possible for your life because you become what you believe." You have to have a big vision for your life to live up to your highest potential.

Level Up Your Day to Day

The first way to expand your vision is to level up your day-to-day routines. Humans are creatures of habit. We do the same thing, the same way over and over again. We take the same route to work unless there is an accident that forces us to divert to a new route. We eat at the same restaurants, shop at the same stores, and go to the same places for fun and recreation. There are people in my life who no matter where we eat I could order their meal for them without even asking them. They eat the same thing all the time!

From your career to romantic relationships, maintaining the same routine without deviation can lead to complacency. Complacency leads to being in a rut.

Yet we like routine. It makes us feel safe, secure, and confident. That routine, that sameness, keeps your vision small. When you want to expand your vision of what's possible for your life, look at the day-to-day things that you do that are on autopilot.

To start, make a list of the things that you do most days.

Where do you eat? What do you eat? Who do you eat with?

What do you do in the evenings after work? How do you spend your weekends?

These are just some examples. You can find additional questions in the appendix on page 206.

Once you have your list of routines, spend some time reflecting on each individual

Expand Your Vision to Expand Your Life

item. Ask yourself, "How can I level this up?" Identify those places where you've settled into a routine that limits your vision.

I was sitting at my desk when a text message comes through. It's from Jamie.

"What's up?" she asks.

"Hi," I reply.

"How are you doing?" Jamie answers back.

"Good. You?"

"I'm good. Anything new your way?" Jamie asks.

"Nope. Not really," I say.

Jamie agrees, "Yea, me neither."

I have had this text exchange with Jamie several times a week for months. There's the occasional complaint about her husband or coworkers, but in general this is how the conversations went. Jamie and I have been friends for fifteen years. There are seasons where we don't talk much for years. There are other seasons where we catch up every few months. For some reason, during this season Jamie and I chatted frequently. The problem was the surface-level nature of our conversations. I don't enjoy talking for the sake of talking. I like to have meat and substance when socializing.

I wondered, "Why is Jamie regularly initiating these no-conversation conversations with me all the sudden?"

It turns out she was bored. Jamie has a career, a husband, a house, three kids, and a dog. She has checked off all the major hallmarks of success. As she has settled into the routine of the American dream, she has found herself bored.

This type of boredom is scary. If you are bored for the night, you can go to the movies and take a walk around the park. What do you do when you're bored in life? You shake up your routine. This exercise in leveling up your day-to-day life will help you do that.

As you break the autopilot cycle, you open yourself up to new ideas and inspirations. Your imagination is stretched. If you're stretching your imagination every single day, your vision will be stretched as well.

On the other hand, when you're so caught up in what you always do, you stop thinking about it. You stop thinking about where you want to go for dinner. Your car just automatically takes you to restaurant you always frequent. You stop thinking about what you want out of life in general. You live life according to your status quo. You allow boredom to creep in.

When this happens you relinquish control of the wheel steering your life and allow the autopilot to kick in. Being on autopilot is not visioning. Visioning requires you to think, to see, and to believe on purpose. Being a stickler for habits is keeping your vision small.

Routines can also be helpful. For example, having a specific routine or schedule for exercising can be advantageous because it stops you from thinking whether you should work out today or wait until tomorrow. Removing that decision point can help you stick to your workout goals.

If your routines are purposeful, productive, and inspiring, you're in a great place. If you want to look for ways to level up your inspiring routines, you can, but focus most of your energy on the routines that have you in a rut. Focus on leveling up those routines that are unproductive or stifling your vision.

If you are complacent in everyday life, you are at risk for living a small life. When you constantly question what else each experience you encounter can be, you position yourself to live a bigger life.

Set Long-Term Goals

It's pretty common to establish New Year's resolutions every January. People across the globe declare what they want the new year to be. Generally they think about what they wish to create in their lives for the next twelve months. We're really good at setting short-term goals.

You need short-term goals, but you also need long-term goals. I challenge you to train your vision to see further into the future. Create long-term goals for yourself.

Travel three years into the future. What do you see? Where are you? Who are you with? What have you accomplished?

Travel five years into the future. What do you see now? What else have you been able to accomplish?

Finally travel ten years into the future. What do you see now?

This is a great exercise for you to journal. Imagine that you have a time machine and can travel into your future. What do you most want to see there? Journal your desired future using the present tense. Begin your sentences with "I am" or "I have."

We tend to overestimate what we can do in a year, which leaves us discouraged. We tend to underestimate what we can achieve in five years, which leaves us stuck because we don't realize that we could really have a whole new life five years from now.

Marcus and I dated when I was in college. When I was pulling all-nighters to barely make it through calculus, Marcus was playing video games. He said he was taking a break. It was the break that never ended.

I used to tell him, "If you do something different today, in five years you'll be somewhere else. But if you keep doing what you're doing, in five years you'll be right where you are."

Eight years after I graduated from college, Marcus came to visit me in Houston. Guess where his life was? It was right where it was eight years prior. There was no progress. There was no growth. He was doing absolutely nothing! In fact he had digressed. He was diagnosed with diabetes. He was on disability because he couldn't stand for long periods of time. And he was working a very part-time job.

My life on the other hand has grown. I've bathed in the sun on beautiful beaches in Mexico, Honduras, and Trinidad and Tobago. From Niagara Falls in Canada to Christ the Redeemer in Brazil, I've seen some of this world's most magnificent sights. I've bought multiple rental houses to build my net worth. I've lost weight, grown closer to God, and so much more. I don't say that to brag. I say it to show you that you can accomplish a lot in five years. However, if you keep doing what you're doing now, in five years you'll be right where you are today at best. At worst you will have digressed.

You can accomplish a lot in five years. You can completely change your life around. You can make a career shift. You can graduate from college. You can meet a partner and start a family. There's so much available to you. When you want to expand your vision, you want to think beyond just the next twelve months.

I teach people in my Transform Your Year program to ladder their goals back up. For example, if you're thinking, "I want to buy a house in three years," then you know you need to be doing some things at the one-year mark to be able to buy the house at the three-year mark. Whether it's saving for a down payment or cleaning up your credit, there are smaller milestones to hit along the way.

That's another reason why it is important to think long term. You might not be adequately prepared for goals you'll have in three years if you're only focused on the next twelve months.

You want your short-, mid-, and long-term goals to work in concert with each other. Make sure that your short-term goals actually ladder back up to your long-term goals.

Initially I thought real-estate investing was my five-year plan. I wanted to be ready. I didn't want to say, "In five years I want to start investing in real estate," yet when the five years rolled around, I would have no knowledge of real-estate investing and no money to put down on a property. If I wanted to be investing in five years, I needed to get my knowledge and my money together now. I needed to start working on some things in the short term so that I would be ready in the long term.

I wanted to be buying in five years, not learning in five years. But you know what? When you start learning what you need to learn and taking action on that learning, sometimes it goes faster than you thought. I bought my first rental house within five months. My five-year plan turned into my five-month plan because I aimed to be prepared for the five-year mark. I didn't realize it was doable before then, but it was.

It's to your advantage to think about where you want to be in the future, because when you start to do the things today to get you to where you want to be in the future, it might go faster than you thought possible. Your life can be transformed in five months instead of five years.

Expose Yourself to New Things

The third thing that you can do to expand your vision is expose yourself to new things. Purposefully try out new things. It can be as simple as watching a new TV show or taking a class on something that's interesting to you. You expand your vision by exposing yourself to new things and exposing yourself to new people.

I've spent nearly a decade in corporate America; that experience transformed my vision of what is possible. The first time I ate at an upscale restaurant was in corporate America. A vendor my department outsourced work to visited Houston to meet the team in person. Because they were earning a heavy revenue from us, they treated the team to lunch at a nice, upscale restaurant. It was so upscale that they didn't even give you to-go bags. I really wanted to take my fish home with me. It was the most decadent fish paired with sweet potato ravioli. It was delicious, but I was just too embarrassed to ask for a to-go bag. It was that upscale. I had never eaten at that kind of restaurant before. But now I can treat myself to those restaurants because I've been exposed to them. I realize

Expand Your Vision to Expand Your Life

I enjoy that upscale experience. I can't do it all the time, but it has opened up my eyes to the possibility. I learned that I have options available to me that I do not even realize. You do as well.

Expose yourself to new ideas, people, and environments as often as possible.

Bring Your Vision to Life

I'm driving through one of the most affluent neighborhoods in my area. There's a stirring in my soul. I'm a bit emotional. Butterflies are dancing in my stomach, and my heart starts to twinkle. I think I'm in love. This is where I belong.

I pull in front of an awe-inspiring house. It has to be about six thousand square feet. Compare that to my current fourteen-hundred-square-foot house. It's a contemporary house with a three-car garage. I park my car on the curb and walk to the oversized front door. I twist the knob, and the door opens.

The stirring in my soul intensifies. The grand foyer is breathtaking. Off to the side is a home office with double French doors. This is where I'll do my life's work.

I fill the room with a desk, chairs, file cabinets, and inspiring photos—in my imagination, that is.

On to the kitchen. I circle the island, while my fingers glaze the tan granite countertop. I open the oven door. I can prepare wholesome meals in this kitchen.

Next to the kitchen is a wine cellar. I don't keep alcohol in the house, but this is pretty cool.

I move to the movie room and close the door behind me. I want to see how dark this room really gets. Oh wow! There's a mini refrigerator and microwave built in! Popcorn and beverages on deck!

In the master bedroom, there's a huge bathroom. The shower is the largest shower I've ever seen in a single-family house, and it has two shower heads. I've heard of his-and-hers sinks, but his-and-hers shower heads—totally new concept.

There's a huge family room upstairs and a barbecue pit outside. This house is beautiful.

I love looking at houses that I cannot afford (yet). I can walk in the door and pretend that this house is mine. I can see myself living there and enjoying life there, because I am there. I'm literally walking through the door, and I can see me walking through it as my door.

It's so important to bring your visions to life. Experiencing your dream firsthand transfers the dream from your head to your heart.

Of course I can live in my dream home. I'm literally standing in it.

Some people have small vision because they simply can't imagine a bigger life. Perhaps they stopped believing years ago. If you put yourself in your vision, if only for a moment, you convince yourself that this is possible. You invite the dream into your spirit.

It's hard to believe in something that isn't as if it is. Bringing the vision to life supports you in believing in your vision. It strengthens your connection to the vision. It stirs up something in you. And you just cannot help but keep moving toward it.

Double Your Vision

Expand Your Vision to Expand Your Life

Pause for a moment, and think about your grand vision for life.

If you're like most people, you thought up a teeny- weeny vision. Maybe it was two steps above your current reality.

Even when someone says to think about the greatest thing you could achieve in life most people still tend to stifle the vision. They filter it through their minds that are congested with doubts and fears before they even open their mouths to affirm it.

Go back to the vision you saw a few moments ago. What would that same vision look like if you doubled it?

Double your vision so that you know you're not playing small. You want to be sure you're going after the biggest vision possible.

Instead of a $100,000 house, the vision becomes a $200,000 house. Instead of one family vacation a year, the vision becomes two family vacations a year. Instead of a joyful life, the vision becomes a double dose of joyfulness.

Note: You can't double your husbands or your wives; it's illegal. And you might not want to double your kids because it would just be crazy.

A double vision may not be what's most fulfilling to you. I don't want you to chase things that do not matter to you. I've had well-meaning people tell me I was playing too small, and it was frustrating as heck. My vision isn't your vision. Your mother's vision isn't your vision. Nobody has the right vision for you, but you.

Doubling your vision is more of a sniff test. This is not about consuming more and more just for consumption's sake. This is about making sure that you're not selling your vision short because of fear or feelings of unworthiness. Go for what you really want out of life. Ask for double.

In this next step, I want to walk through my favorite Bible verse. I realize this isn't a biblical or Christian book; however, I invite you to continue reading. The context is applicable to your vision. I mentioned previously it is important to expose yourself to new ideas and concepts. If you are not a believer in the Bible, here is an opportunity to do so.

My favorite Bible verse is Habakkuk 2:3:

> The vision is yet for the appointed time.
> It speaks to the end and shall not lie.
> Though it tarry, wait for it.
> For it will certainly come and shall not be late.

Let's break this down!
"The vision": The first two words are so powerful when you're thinking about your vision. The vision. They are powerful words because it could say "a vision," but it doesn't. It says, "the vision." What's the difference between "a" and "the"?

If I said *a* car has four wheels, what comes to mind?

If I said *the* car has four wheels, would that conjure a different meaning?

A car is a hypothetical car. It could or it could not exist. I don't know where a car is located. But *the* car is a real, specific, tangible car. It's probably parked in the garage.

The vision that you have is not hypothetical. It is real. It is specific. Sometimes we have a vision and then start to question ourselves. We think, "What was I thinking? Who am I to have that vision?"

"The vision" tells you that you don't have to question or doubt your vision because it's not a hypothetical vision. It is a real physical vision.

"The vision is for the appointed time":

There is a specific time that this vision is called to come into creation and manifestation. The vision is for the appointed time.

"It speaks to the end":

A lot of times when we get a glimpse of the vision of what we want our lives to become, we want it to come to fruition right away. We get discouraged and beat ourselves up because we have this vision and don't yet have it in our lives. But the ideation of the vision is the beginning of the journey. The moment you think up the vision, you're at the beginning. Yet the manifestation of the vision, speaks to the end. You have to be prepared to take a journey to accomplish what you want to accomplish. There is no need to get discouraged when you're still at the beginning. You have to acknowledge and know where you are.

The manifestation of the vision is at the end of the journey, and you're at the beginning. Understand that so that you don't get discouraged. Be prepared for the journey.

"It shall not lie":

In chapter 3 I said your purpose isn't misleading you; it wants you as much as you want it. The same can be said for your vision because your vision is a part of your purpose. Or else you probably wouldn't be envisioning it. Your vision is not misleading you. It wants you as much as you want it. It's not lying to you. It's truthful and pulling you along. As long as you're willing to walk the journey, the vision is pulling you; it will not lie to you.

"Though it tarry":

Tarry means delays—though the vision delays. Notice it doesn't say "if." It's not if the vision delays. It is when the vision delays because it's going to delay. There are going to be roadblocks and setbacks. There are going to be times where it feels as if nothing's happening. Even though you're taking action, it feels as though you're standing still. The delay will happen. Don't expect it not to happen. There will be delays.
When there is a delay or though it tarries,

"Wait for it."

Your only responsibility is to wait. It doesn't say to give up. It doesn't say to go create another vision. You just have to wait.
I see this all the time. When someone has a vision that is not happening on their timetable, they give up on the vision. I see it especially often with new business owners. One minute they are a coach, the next minute they're a network marketer. And then the next

minute, they're trying out economy sharing. They are all over the place. Why? Because they weren't prepared for the delay. And when it happens, they think they have the wrong vision. Your only responsibility—not if it delays, but when it delays—is to wait.

"Wait for it, for it will certainly come":

Not maybe. Not should be. Not could be. It will certainly come. And it will not be late.

I love that verse. The verse before it, Habakkuk 2:2, says, "Make the vision plain. Write it on the tablet so that he who reads it can run with it." Make your vision plain. Write it down so that you can read it, and run with it.

Sometimes that is my prayer to God: "God, make this vision plain so I can run with it."

Getting Real

Where have you gotten complacent in your daily routines?

_____
_____
_____

Where do you see yourself in three years?

_____
_____
_____

What vision can you bring to life? Get creative. Some ideas: tour a house currently outside your financial reach, test drive your dream car, have a destination-themed dinner party.

_____
_____
_____

What's your double vision? Go back to the third question in the Getting Real section from the previous chapter.

_____
_____
_____

7 *Balance and Boundaries*

If you've picked up this book in search of a life transformation, there's a good chance that somewhere along the way you have failed to establish optimal balance in various areas of your life. There's also a good chance you have failed to set or maintain effective boundaries. Balance and boundaries are critical aspects of living a life you love. They force you to take a proactive stance of what it is you want, what you're willing to give in exchange for those wants, and what guidepost you need to put in place to allow you to achieve those wants.

Let's Start with Balance

What is balance? Life can be grouped into buckets or categories. For example, there is a health bucket, a work/career bucket, and relationship buckets. If you think about all those buckets, balance is making sure that there is something in every bucket that matters to you. Every day we make decisions, intentionally or not, to put our energy, time, money, and affection in certain buckets. Every bucket might get some portion of your resources. Some buckets might get no portion of your resources. Balance is paying attention to where, when, and how you divvy up your resources for life buckets. It is making sure that you're not neglecting some of life's buckets that you care about while putting all your attention into another one of life's buckets.

It's easy to put all of your energy, effort, and attention into one or two buckets, but that's not balance. Not only is it not balance but it's not a good way to create a satisfying or fulfilling life. Having each of these buckets filled is really important for being well-rounded and fulfilled and for enjoying all that life has to offer to you.

What you're doing today is going to create something in your future. Right at this moment, you are traveling on one of life's many roads. If you stay on this road, it's going to take you somewhere. The difference when you purposefully establish balance is in five years you won't end up somewhere and think, "Why am I here? How did I get here?" In five years you have the potential of ending up somewhere that you actually want to be.

Being intentional about how you're living your life is like having a road map to your dream destination. Not being intentional is equivalent to hitchhiking to an unknown destination on the next thing smoking. Anywhere will do. But will it?

We can think about this in basic terms. If you eat whatever you want to eat and never exercise, in five years on this path, you could be twenty, thirty, or fifty pounds overweight.

Eventually you think, "How did I get here?" Well, it's because you didn't have balance five years ago.

You're always creating something. You don't have a choice. You can't turn off your creating mechanism. If you are alive, you are creating. At the end of one year, there are some things that you would have created. Are you going to create what you really want to create, or are you haphazardly going to create any ol' thing?

Another reason why balance is important is because we tend to focus on the big thing. You may have heard the saying that the squeaky wheel gets the grease. The loudest areas of your life tend to get the grease—the grease being your attention.

Monica had an intense passion to grow her blog into a full-time business. She invested heavily in its growth. She put all her free time and energy into the business. As she put it, she was burning the midnight oil. In fact she was burning both ends of the candle.

In the midst of building her dream business, Monica married the love of her life. She continued to work hard on her company, and things were finally starting to take off. She dug in a little deeper. She was on the cusp of breaking through the cocoon and finally seeing her business fly. She was excited. She was focused. She couldn't let up. She could sense she was almost there. She dug in even deeper.

Her marriage, on the other hand, wasn't taking off. It was still sitting on the runway, engines turning. What was supposed to be the honeymoon phase, that critical first year of marriage, was anything but. Monica and her new husband were growing apart.

Monica was neglecting her marriage. She was not paying attention to how much of her resources were allocated to the marriage bucket.

Sometimes this happens. It's evitable, but it's something that should be monitored and adjusted as needed. If Monica had continued down the path she was on for too long, in five years she may have ended up divorced.

Luckily her husband sat her down and let her know she was neglecting the marriage. Monica was able to create balance in her life. Her business continued to flourish, and now so did her marriage.

Like Monica you can't just focus on the squeaky wheel at the expense of other life buckets that you care about.

The choices you make have consequences. There is no right or wrong way to balance your life. Every scenario you can dream up will cost you something. The key is that you want to be okay with the consequences. You don't want to subject yourself to consequences and then later on be regretful, sad, and depressed about it.

For some people it wouldn't be a huge deal if they ended up divorced in exchange for pursuing their dreams or having the career that they really want. We see it all the time. Relationships feel like a hindrance to some people. If it is your conscious choice to choose your dream over your marriage, that is fine.

Monica could have said, "I don't really want to slow down now." She could have chosen to continue putting all into her business and separated from her husband.

Other people want to have a great career, but they also want to have a successful home life and marriage. A divorce or breakup would devastate them.

It is important that you're not just giving all your energy and attention to the wheel that squeaks the loudest. You need to be intentional and purposeful about it. You have to make sure that you're making decisions today that will allow you to have what you want in the future. Paying attention to how you are dividing your resources can help you do that.

Don't let your future be accidental. Be purposeful about it. Know that there are consequences, but make sure that you are okay with where the chips fall. If you're not going to be okay with it, now is the time to adjust your allocations. Now is the time to choose where your chips will fall.

Think about the life that you're living today, and look into the future. Are you okay with what you see? If your future doesn't align with what you really want to create, then it's time for you to look at the road you're traveling right now. What changes do you need to make so that your current direction aligns with your desired future? Be an active participant in your life's unfoldment so that your future has for you what you want.

How Do You Create Balance?

The life-balance wheel is a great exercise to help you identify where you are over- or under allocated in life's buckets. The life-balance wheel that I created has eight categories, or life buckets (you can find on page 202):

1. Physical environment: This represents your home, your car, and the physical, tangible things in your life.
2. Health: This represents your physical health, your weight, your blood pressure, your cholesterol, and all those things that relate to the health and well-being of your physical body.
3. Wealth: These are material possessions, your prosperity, what you are able to afford in terms of lifestyle and resources, and being able to leave something to future generations.
4. Work: Wealth and work are two different things. Work is the actual work that you do day in and day out. It's how you earn your living. You want to rate your work life separately from your wealth, because you might really enjoy your work life, although your wealth might be less than desirable. On the other hand, you might make great money while doing work that bores the life out of you.
5. Play: This is your social life and the things that you do for fun. It covers things such as how often you do make time for fun, how you vacation, and where you go.
6. Relationships: This covers both romantic and platonic.
7. Personal growth: How much time, effort, and energy are you dedicating to growing yourself?
8. Spirituality: How much time, effort, and energy are you dedicating to your spiritual life and needs?

As an important aside, you don't have to accept everything that I have here. You can go through the buffet line and not put everything on your plate. If these aren't the right eight categories for you, you can scratch them out and create the categories that you think belong. If you think you need more categories, you can create a life-balance wheel for yourself or Google other options. Don't feel obligated to follow these eight buckets because this is a part of how you create balance. Identify what those major life buckets are for you—not for Charlene. This balance wheel may work for you, or it may just be a starting place.

Once you're clear on the buckets, go through each one, one by one, and reflect on how you feel about that area. Take for example the health bucket. How satisfied are you with your current health? Think in terms of whatever that means to you. It could be your weight. It could be your energy level. It could be your blood pressure.

On a scale of one to ten, how would you rate your health? Fill that slice of the pie in to represent how satisfied you are with it. Do that for every one of the buckets for your current situation. How satisfied are you right now in each of these areas of your life?

Here are some questions you might want to consider as you complete this exercise:

- How satisfied are you with your current situation?
- How much time and effort are you able to invest in each bucket?
- Are you pursuing all the goals and dreams you have?

Next fill in a second wheel with what your ideal situation is. The idea here is not that you will have a pie slice that is completely full. Your life-balance wheel cannot be 100 percent filled in because everything comes with a sacrifice. You don't want to strive to be perfect. You want to decide what's important to you and at what level would your needs be met. You can't fill the buckets to capacity, but you can fill them to an area that you're comfortable with.

Once you have your current situation and your desired or ideal situation, ask yourself, "What's off?"

What buckets are off? Is one bucket too high? Are you spending too much time or energy on one thing while neglecting something else? Is something that you really care about—like your spirituality—taking the back seat in your life? You may have to make some tough decisions in order to create the balance you desire.

Kyle mentioned to me that he felt there were not enough hours in the day for him to attend church. He was working full time at a hospital and also working on a degree. To create balance and add to his spirituality bucket, he could decide to cut his hours back at school. This would likely push out his graduation. Remember there are consequences no matter the choice you make. Only you can decide what's best for you. If Kyle genuinely wanted to, he could bring his spirituality bucket up to a level he would feel comfortable with by making sacrifices in other areas.

Identify where the gap is, and then create a plan for closing the gap. Give yourself three to six months to see the recalibration of the balance. You should walk away after you do this exercise with specific areas that you want to improve. But they are not going to improve overnight. It takes time to transform your life. Give yourself at least three to six months working at recreating balance for yourself consistently, and then come back and look at this exercise again to see if you're making headway or not. If not, it's okay. Just keep on going.

Share your life-balance worksheet with other people in your life who matter. You might rate your relationship an 80 percent satisfactory level and feel satisfied with that level. But your partner might say that your relationship is at 40 percent and that if something doesn't change, then they are walking out the door. You don't want to do this in a silo because it might not be reflective of what other people who matter to you feel.

Keep in mind, the purpose of this exercise is to make sure that you are creating the life you most want to create. You don't want to be surprised down the line when life isn't how you want it to be. If you think that your current relationship is at a certain level and your partner disagrees, years down the line you might be surprised if they are ready to walk out. Invite important people in your life to provide their own assessment.

Another important thing to note is that the life-balance wheel is not something that you can just do one time and then it's done. It is an evolving wheel. As you evolve, the areas in your life that matter most to you will also evolve.

Setting Boundaries

Boundaries are dividing lines that separate what's acceptable from what's unacceptable. They are the lines that say, "If you cross this line, all hell is going to break loose." Or more simply boundaries are the lines that you are holding people in your life to.

Boundaries help you protect yourself mentally, physically, spiritually, and emotionally. When you set boundaries, you are defining the rules of engagement for your life. Setting boundaries honors who you are. It honors what you want and deserve. It gives you control over your life.

Setting healthy boundaries protects your self-esteem. If you allow people to treat you a certain way, those who don't honor you may tell you negative things about yourself and treat you badly. They will tell you that you're not good enough, pretty enough, or wise enough. You may be inclined to believe them, which diminishes your self-worth.

Setting boundaries improves your relationship with others by giving them the guidelines of what they can and cannot do and say to you. If everyone understands and agrees these are the right boundaries, then the relationships can flourish.

When you don't set and maintain effective boundaries, it gives others the opportunity to control your life. It opens the door for others to manipulate, mistreat, and dishonor you. You give away control when you fail to set boundaries with other people.

Setting boundaries also allows you to create the balance you desire. Having boundaries with your boss can help your home life. Having boundaries with your husband or your kids can help your spirituality. Being able to set healthy boundaries helps you create the right balance.

How do you set boundaries? A really simple exercise is to take a sheet of paper, draw a vertical line down the center, and then draw a horizontal line at the top. On the left-hand side, write, "Things I say yes to," and on the right-hand side write, "Things I say no to." Write in those things you say yes to and the things you say no to.

A good starting point is to go back to your balance wheel. Were there some areas that were out of balance? What are the things you need to say yes and no to in order to create your ideal balance?

Think about the things that are giving you headaches right now. What things are causing you exhaustion or feelings of sadness? Is there something you should be saying no to?

Are you experiencing any conflict in your relationships? If so, is it possible a boundary is being crossed?

Consider your goals and where you want to be. What do you need to say yes to and what do you need to say no to in order to accomplish your goals? For example, if you want to lose weight, then you might say no to cheeseburgers and yes to clean foods.

A lot of times when we think about boundaries, we think about them as it relates to romantic relationships. We think about a partner crossing the line. But it's imperative to set boundaries in all the major buckets of your life. You must also set boundaries with yourself—the things you do, eat, or say.

Once you have set your boundaries, communicate them to your friends, family, and colleagues as necessary. You have to let people know what your boundaries are.

The first time that someone crosses the line, tell that person. You might say when someone is late, "I value people being on time, and I would appreciate if you would be on time. And if you're not going to be, you need to let me know."

A lot of times, the first time someone crosses our boundary, we excuse his or her behavior. "Oh, maybe she just got stuck in traffic."

But then it becomes a pattern, and either you're too afraid to speak up because you've let it happen for so long or you are so flustered and frustrated that when it does finally come to a head, you're blowing up.

I've had blowups with friends over being late. They had been showing up late for so long, sometimes an hour or longer. I finally blew up, and the friendship has never been the same. It doesn't have to get to that point. Inform people the first time they cross your boundary. If they can't respect it, they can't be in your life.

You might be reading this thinking, "I have not set healthy boundaries in my life." It's never too late to set healthy boundaries in your life.

Sometimes we tell ourselves, "I didn't say anything the last time, so if I say something now, I'm going to look flaky."

That's not true. It doesn't matter how many times something has happened before. If it was outside your boundaries, it is perfectly okay to tell people. If you change your mind about what is or isn't acceptable, it is also okay to tell people, "I've changed my mind. I have a new viewpoint. That is no longer acceptable for me."

Follow the SOAR model for setting effective boundaries in your life:

SET clear, specific boundaries. Don't be ambiguous about what you want and need.

OPENLY communicate those boundaries. Never hesitate or wait for an invitation.

Balance and Boundaries

Communicate them early and as often as needed.

ASK for your boundaries to be honored. Get a commitment that you have been heard and that your boundaries will be respected.

REMOVE anyone from your life who refuses to oblige or who repeatedly crosses your boundaries.

You are protecting your space—mentally, physically, emotionally, financially, and spiritually—when you establish boundaries. When you allow someone to cross them, it's like giving the opposing army permission to infiltrate your front line unopposed. Don't allow your boundaries to be crossed without repercussions.

FROM CATERPILLAR TO BUTTERFLY

Getting Real

What area of your life is out of balance? Why?

_____
_____
_____

What actions will you take to create the balance you desire?

_____
_____
_____

What boundaries in your life are being crossed? What will you do to reinforce them?

_____
_____
_____

Balance and Boundaries Meditation

Take a deep breath in. Exhale. Read the following affirmations. You can say these out loud or simply in your head.

I am balanced and I set healthy boundaries.

I honor the boundaries I set for myself.

I honor other people's boundaries.

Everyone in my life honors my boundaries.

I choose my own future.

I always communicate my true boundaries.

I am in control of my own life.

I require everyone in my life to honor my boundaries.

I honor all of life's buckets that are important to me.

I live a healthy life.

I live a balanced life of my choosing.

I create the balance that is most meaningful to me and my goals.

I am creating the future of my choosing.

Everyone in my life treats me the way I want to be treated.

I'm creating my best future possible.

Download free meditation audio at
fromcaterpillarstobutterflies.com/specialgift

8 Know Your Values

Most people never think about what their values are. It's not something that's top of mind, which can be problematic in creating a life you love. When you're going through life and not paying attention to how your decisions and actions line up with your values, then you can end up down the wrong path. When you are not aligned with your values, you can lose feelings of satisfaction and fulfillment in your life.

Your values are your GPS—Goal Positioning System. They position you to take hold of your biggest dreams with integrity, character, and poise. Your values make sure you're actually pursing your goals and not someone else's.

Values are defined as the relative worth or importance of something.[9] They are the things that are important to you in your life as a whole. When I talk about values in this chapter, I'm talking about your core values. It is possible to value a lot of things, and we do. But we build our lives around our core values.

In chapter 7 I talked about the balance wheel and how we balance eight life buckets. There are things within each of those buckets or categories that we value. But at the center of the balance wheel, at the core, are values that impact every area of your life.

Those are your core values. Your core values determine several things:

- How you spend your time, money, and resources
- What you will or won't do
- What you will or won't say
- How you treat other people and how you require other people to treat you
- What you take a stand for and what you are quiet about

Everything that is of you and from you is born from your core values. It's important that you know what they are. Most people never put a name to their values. Toward the end of this chapter, you will have an opportunity to do just that.

When you truly understand what your values are, you will be able to design your life around what matters most to you. You will make better decisions as you are able to assess quickly if something aligns with your values or not. You'll understand your why. Knowing your why is critical to creating a life you love.

---

[9] "Value." Merriam-Webster. Accessed June 01, 2017. https://www.merriam-webster.com/dictionary/value.

Being able to articulate what you value will give you peace of mind, clarity, and alignment in your pursuits.

As a corporate marketer, I can almost guarantee that someone somewhere is in a meeting or boardroom discussing you at this very moment. They're discussing what your values are. They're mapping out what needs you have in this season of your life. They're hypothesizing what season of life you're headed into and anticipating what your needs, values, and wants will be once there. For good or for bad, someone is vested in who you are, what you value, and what you need. Are you vested in your own values and needs? How often do you take time to identify and reassess those values, needs, and wants?

How Do You Know What Your Values Are?

In order to live your best life, you need to be a person who honors their values. In order to honor your values, you have to know what they are. You don't want to be someone who says they want certain things for their life but nobody can tell. No one can tell because they don't act like it matters to them. They don't move like they want it. They dishonor their values.

If you don't know what your values are or if you cannot act in accordance with them, it will be difficult to create a fulfilling life. When you don't know your values, you may

- be more inclined to make bad decisions;
- focus on the wrong things and people;
- not walk your talk;
- be wishy-washy (have a weak yes/no muscle);

- be swayed and tempted with what everyone else is doing or saying; and
- try to keep up with the Joneses and chase what's cool.

Your values are directing your life right now. For a lot of people this happens below the surface. It's not something they are mindful of. Knowing what values are directing your life is important as you work to transform the life you have into the life you love. It's so important that this chapter is geared toward facilitating your understanding of your core values. The questions throughout are designed to help you learn more about what you value.

What makes you happy and brings you joy?

_____
_____
_____

What frustrates you? Why?

_____
_____
_____

Where do you spend your time and money? Where do you want to be spending your time and money?

_____
_____
_____

Know Your Values

One of my rental properties had termites. When I found out, I started to stress out. When I think about all the things that I worry about, I worry about my tenants. I worry about making sure that they are safe. Whether it is termites or a leaky roof, I worry about their well-being. That worry tells me that I value providing a safe environment for my tenants. I value being a good person who takes care of other people.

What do you worry about repeatedly?

_____
_____
_____

Think of some of your accomplishments. What are you most proud of?

_____
_____
_____

What brings you a sense of fulfillment?

_____
_____
_____

Who do you admire and why?

_____
_____
_____

I used to sit next to Mark at work. He was a good guy. We had a friendly, professional relationship. Yet, he irked me for some reason. The mere sight of him irritated me and I felt horrible about it. Over time I realized what drove my dislike of him.

Mark was living in Texas. He had a house in Florida that he claimed a homestead exemption on. The homestead exemption is a tax break for your primary residence. In other words you have to live in the house to claim the exemption. Mark was doing a dishonest thing by claiming the tax credit.

On top of that he had a second house that he hadn't paid the mortgage on in several years despite receiving rental income from a tenant. The lender wanted the house back. Mark hired a lawyer to help him fight the bank and keep the house. Yet, he was earning revenue on the house every single month. That just didn't seem right to me.

I don't want that to sound judgmental—maybe it is—but ultimately what I realized is that he doesn't share my values. Like I said he was a cool guy; sometimes even funny. So why was I so standoffish with him? The answer is that he doesn't have the same values as I have. My values are doing the right thing, being honorable, repaying my debts, and not claiming exemptions that aren't for me. I'm a stickler for the rules most of the time. Those are my values.

A lot of times when we have certain feelings about other people, we either judge ourselves for feeling them or we think that there's something wrong with the other person. The truth is it's a clue to who we are and what we value. Paying attention to

Know Your Values

what you like and dislike can help you pinpoint exactly what it is that you value.

It's also important to note that it's okay that we all don't have the same values. Just like our fingerprints are all different, no two people are the same. My values are my values. Your values are your values. You don't have to let those differences define the relationship as long as there is mutual respect. When you understand this, it takes the pressure off you and those in your life.

Who do you dislike and why?

_____
_____
_____

What's the biggest argument you've had? How was it resolved?

_____
_____
_____

What issues do you take a stand for?

_____
_____
_____

     I've heard of hostile work environments but this one took the cake. I was in a very tense environment with a boss who was a bit of a bully. She had a short temper and could often be heard yelling at the team. She was also known for name calling and threatening to fire her direct reports. When she wasn't yelling or name calling, her intimidation tool of preference was performance write-ups.

Leah waited until my boss Rebecca had left the office for the day. She pulled me to the side and said, "Charlene, you really should talk to Steph about moving to his team." That's how bad it was.

Leah and other coworkers were trying to get me out of that crazy situation. They were urging me to put up a fight. Everything from speaking with Rebecca's boss to recording our conversations was suggested to me. But I didn't want to fight. It would just create a bigger mess.

I didn't want to create more drama because regardless of the outcome, I didn't want to be on Rebecca's team. Either I was going to leave the company or I was going to change teams, but I wasn't going to stay on her team. There was no reason to fight because I didn't want the consolation prize; Rebecca as a boss.

What are some of the arguments that you will not fight? Why?

_____
_____
_____

When have you gone out of your way to help someone? Why?

_____
_____
_____

Know Your Values

What are some of the biggest sacrifices you've made for others?

_____

_____

_____

What decisions do you regret? What decisions would you make again in a heartbeat?

_____

_____

_____

What do you feel drawn to?

_____

_____

_____

What things, people, or events do you pull away from?

_____

_____

_____

As you reflect on these questions and even perhaps additional questions I haven't posed, what are some of the common themes that run through your answers?

FROM CATERPILLAR TO BUTTERFLY

One of the themes that runs through my answers is peace. I value peace and stress-free environments. That shows up in my work environments. It also shows up in my financial environment. Building wealth is important to me because it creates peace of mind.

What are some of the values that keep coming up for you? Take three to five of the most common attributes and list them here. These are likely your core values.

1.
2.
3.
4.
5.

What do you think about this list? How does it make you feel? Do you resonate with the words on your core values list?

Another technique for uncovering your core values is to ask other people who know you well what they think your core values are. Don't ask leading questions. Avoid asking questions such as, "Would you say I value family?" Simply ask, "What would you say my values are?"

Ask a few different people. Search for the key themes in their responses.

When you hear what other people say your values how that makes you feel. Do those values resonate with you?

_____
_____
_____

Are you surprised by what other people think your values are?

_____
_____
_____

Why would people have the impression that those are your values (good or bad)?

_____
_____
_____

Prioritize Your Values

Next take your core values and prioritize them. What are your highest values?

Sometimes we have a hard time making decisions because there is more than one value at stake. For example, I value building wealth, but I also value financial stability. I value having a cushion in the bank. I don't want to be stressed about money every month. Living below my means is important to me. Sometimes these two values compete against each other. I might have an opportunity to invest in something that can help me build wealth, but that means taking money out of my cushion.

At some point your values will compete with each other. It's important that you not only know what your values are but also in what order you value them.

Rank your values, one being the highest core value and five being the lowest core value:

1.

2.

3.

4.

5.

Notice the Shift

It's not uncommon for your values or their order to shift. There are years where I invested heavily in building wealth. Other years I prioritized paying down debt.

Obviously as your life shifts, your values may also shift. For example, a single, childless woman might value career over family. When she has a family of her own, family may increase on her prioritization list. Yet if she doesn't shift her behaviors and decisions, she may end up putting career and money above her family.

Pay attention to when your values shift, and make sure to adjust your actions accordingly.

Choose Wisely

When you are forced to choose between your core values, choose the one that is the highest value. Always act in accordance to your highest values. When you are able to do that on a consistent basis, then your life will be more fulfilling and more satisfying. You will live with fewer regrets. You will ask the question "How did I get here?" less often. Choosing your highest values enables you to be proud of who you are even when things don't go right because you know that you chose your values.

Knowing what your values are and keeping them in the forefront of your mind is critical for creating the life that you want to have.

Know Your Needs

In addition to core values, you also have core needs. I'm not just talking about the need for shelter and food. You also have needs for your mental, spiritual, and emotional health and stability.

Similar to values we rarely put a name to our core needs. This makes it difficult to identify when those needs aren't being met. Know your core needs.

Go back to the life buckets in chapter 7. In each of those areas, identify your core needs. Focus on the key three to five needs. What do you absolutely need in that bucket, and what does it look like to have that need met?

For example, in a romantic relationship, one of my core needs is to feel secure. I need to know that we're both in it completely. It's not a fling. I need to feel safe to be vulnerable, to love freely, and to give 100 percent.

What that looks like to me is being first in his life after God. It looks like not ignoring text messages and phone calls for hours on end. It looks like adequate investments of time and energy.

Sometimes our needs aren't being met, but we don't realize it. We know something is off, but we're not sure what. We might even start to think it's us. Perhaps we're "tripping".

Robert routinely ignored my text messages and phone calls for hours on end, but I would see him on social media commenting on pictures and interacting with others. It seemed so trivial. Should I end a relationship because he didn't respond as promptly as I would have liked?

Yes, texting habits in and of themselves are trivial. But those were the symptoms. When I looked at the bigger picture, one of my core needs wasn't being met. I never felt safe or secure with him because he never put me first.

Whether it's a career or a relationship, your core needs must be met for you to create a life you love. Don't underthink your feelings. The issues you have in and of themselves might be trivial, but if they represent a bigger issue, pay attention.

Ending a relationship because he took too long to respond to my texts may sound stupid, but if it represents a core need not being met, it's not stupid. Staying in a relationship that doesn't met my needs is settling. And settling is stupid.

When you understand your core values and needs, you will be able to discern whether you are settling or compromising. If you find you are acting outside your core values and needs, it's time to recalibrate your life and relationships. Get in alignment with your core values, and work to ensure your core needs are being met in every area of your life.

Getting Real

Where are your behaviors, thoughts, and so on not in alignment with your values?

_____
_____
_____

What do you need to do to live in accordance to your highest values?

_____
_____
_____

Where are your core needs not being met?

_____
_____
_____

9 Manifest Your Heart's Desires

It's likely that when you think about transforming your life, you're specifically thinking of new things you'd like to call forth into your life. We've talked about growing into the person you need to be to achieve things you have yet to achieve. We've also talked about expanding your vision so that you see the grandest future possible for you. In this chapter let's talk about some of the tools that will support you in manifesting your heart's desire in this next season of your life.

The Myth

When I was a young girl, I used to love Mase. Mase was a rapper with Bad Boy. He had such a baby face with cute dimples. One of my favorite songs from him was a feature with the R and B group Total.

I loved Mase. I had a giant poster of him on my bedroom wall. I thought about that man daily. I visualized being with him. I kissed him on the lips (on the poster). For years I was obsessed with Mase. He was my boyfriend in my head.

I've heard a lot about thought becoming things. "Just think about what you want with strong emotion repeatedly, and you will manifest it," the experts say.

Yet my thoughts about Mase did not become things. I have never even met the man. I bet you too can think of times where your thoughts, fantasies, and expectations just weren't met.

"Thoughts become things" is a myth. If you believe you can just think your dreams into existence, you will end up wasting a lot of time and staying right where you are. Thoughts do not become things all by themselves. Thoughts backed by action have the strong potential to become things.

Take Radical Action

Radical action will be your best friend when it comes to creating a life you love. There's no fairy godmother to prepare you for the ball. There's no bibbidi-bobbidi-boo at the command of some magical wand. It is you being willing and able to put one foot in front of the other over and over again.

Getting started is the most important thing you can do to manifest your heart's desires. Once you start moving, new paths will become visible to you. You cannot simply imagine what you want and—poof!—it appears. There's no genie in a bottle here.

Your action is your not-so-secret weapon.

Robert Frost so famously said in "The Road Not Taken," "Yet knowing how way leads on to way, I doubted if I should ever come back."

Way leads on to way. Ideas lead on to new ideas. Goals lead to new goals. Progress leads on to progress. And dreams lead on to new dreams.

Standing still does not lead on to way. Circling the mountain does not lead on to way. Thinking and planning without acting does not lead on to progress or dreams or visions.

Your action is the impetus. Have you ever tried to grab a piece of thread from a clothing item? You pick at it and you pick at it, but you just can't grasp it. Finally you seize it and pull it back. That stubborn piece of thread now glides so smoothly as the sewing is quickly unraveled. The thread breaks before you completely unravel it. And so you start the process of picking at it again until it reluctantly gives way and begins to glide once more.

Manifesting your goals is a bit like that piece of thread. It requires you first to take action to seize even just the smallest opportunity. Things start to come together at times faster than you ever imagined. And then you reach a plateau and start the process all over again.

The key words being "you start."

You don't even have to be perfect. In fact you won't be perfect. You will stumble. You will get off track. You will take breaks. You will put your dreams on the back burner.

You will eat the cake, skip the workout, and miss the session. You will start the day late and end early.

Your perfection isn't required. Your footsteps are. Obviously the more you stay on track and the fewer breaks you take, the quicker your results. Taking radical action and always returning when you find yourself out of action will get you to your dream destination in due time.

Find and Fund Your Opportunities

I had an opportunity to speak at a local women's organization. It was my first speaking engagement. It was a great experience. I built my confidence and reaffirmed my gift.

I had an opportunity to go on a mission trip to Haiti to visit orphanages and spend time with amazing children. I've invested in real estate. I've traveled the world. I've written a book.

No one came to me and said, "Hey, Charlene, come speak at our organization."

No one said, "Hey, Charlene, let's go to Haiti."

No one said, "Let's go to London, Charlene."

I found the women's group, and I sent them an e-mail asking to speak during one of their monthly meetings. I found the trip to Haiti on my church's website, and I sponsored myself. No one told me to write this book. Likewise, no one is paying for the expenses of writing this book. I am. Over and over again, I have found my own opportunities and then funded them.

You have to be willing to find and fund your opportunities. Sometimes you fund your opportunities with money. Other times you fund them with time, courage, or sleepless nights. Nevertheless, you have to contribute something.

When I decided to become a real-estate investor, I went to the same event multiple times because it was free. I joined three different organizations about real-estate investing in my area. I read all the books I could get my hands on and took copious notes. I did that for weeks. Sure enough, in due time, I was able to buy my first property. It wasn't because the opportunity to buy a rental house fell into my lap. It wasn't because I sat at home visualizing it and dreaming about it. It was because I was learning, studying, and taking action. I persisted. And then I had to pay for the house as well. There was no investor. I am my own investor.

Manifesting is creating. The way that you create what you want is, you find it and you fund it. You learn. You persist, you take action, and you have a spirit of discipline and consistency. That is how you manifest your heart's desires. You just don't give up.

There's a debilitating fear when it comes to funding the vision. What it boils down to is that we value money more than we value our transformation and dreams. So we keep our money and forgo our dreams. Money is tangible. I can see it, touch it, feel it, and count it. How do I count my transformation?

Holding on to your money is a false sense of security. Your real security is in your ability to grow consistently.

In pursuit of my vision, I maxed out credit cards. I took money out of my 401(k). I've emptied my savings account. What I have

come to learn is that money always comes back. It's the cycle of life.
    You spend money.
    You earn money.
    You give money.
    You receive money.

    I'm not telling you to be fiscally irresponsible. I'm simply saying you cannot be afraid to invest in your dream life. I have accepted that I have to let the money go when it wants to go so that it can come when I want it to come. It always comes back. Do your dreams always come back is the question.

    It would be nice if an opportunity simply fell into your lap. Or so you think. But the truth is if you were given a chance to be a part of something you had no knowledge in and made no investment in, you would more than likely squander it.

    You think you want it to be handed to you, but if it is handed to you, you will not fully appreciate it. Your vision requires your time and money. Your transformation requires your tears and sacrifice. You have to put some skin in the game of your own dream life. There's no other way around it. Or else you will have the opportunity of a lifetime, and it will slip through your fingers.

    Don't wait for opportunities to live a life you love to find you. Take the ownership of finding opportunities that can transform your life. If you are always finding and funding your opportunities, you can't help but create a life you love.

Listen to Your Intuition

    One afternoon I was driving in my car. I was on a three-lane street. The left lane turned left only. The middle lane turned left or went straight. The right lane went straight. I was in the far-left lane because I wanted to turn left. There was a car in front of me, but there was no car in the adjacent lane, which also turned left. I decided I was going to get in the second lane. Something told me not to. Something said, "Don't get over there."

"Why not? There is no one over there," I questioned.

Seconds later—*bam*!

I got hit by the car that was previously in front of me.

Have you ever had a "something told me" experience? There is a knowing in our spirit sometimes that we don't listen to. A part of it is because we're groomed and taught from a young age how to use our critical minds. We're taught how to deduce, analyze, count, and take tests. We're taught how to think, but we're not taught how to nurture our spirit minds. A lot of times when the spirit has some information for us, we start analyzing it and questioning it. More often than not, we don't see physical manifestations of the issue.

I didn't see any reason why I shouldn't switch lanes. I followed my mind and not my spirit. And I got hit.

The spirit knows something that the mind doesn't know at times. Leaning on your intuition or spirit self is critical to manifesting your heart's desires.

Leverage Tools

Several tools are available to you as you work to manifest your heart's desires. Here are some of my favorites.

Journaling

Journaling is a great activity to help you get past your critical mind. When you allow your thoughts to flow without thinking about them, you can get to the heart of what you feel and want.

When I'm feeling stuck or confused about my vision, I will journal "What I really, really want is…" I write whatever comes up for me. As you endeavor to manifest your heart's desires, it's critical to stay in tune with those desires. If you lose sense of what you really, *really* want, it will be nearly impossible to manifest it.

Journaling is also good for reminding yourself of who you are, what you're made of, and who God is. I started journaling years ago because I wanted to know if God answers prayers. It was a faith-building exercise. Whether it's faith in God or faith in yourself, journaling can remind you of past victories, which will build your confidence in your current aspirations.

Brainstorming

Obstacles are going to come up. It will look as though there's no way forward. You might be inclined to believe that the vision is dead. This is where brainstorming can be a dream saver. Similar to journaling, brainstorming is jotting down all the potential solutions that come up for you without judgment. You want to get as many ideas as possible down. Once you have exhausted all solutions, look over your list. Circle the top three or four viable solutions, and explore further.

Brainstorming is a great tool to help you stretch your imagination and remove perceived obstacles that aren't actually impeding your efforts. Explore new options and avenues to make the progress that you want to make.

Vision Boards

A vision board is a board covered with visual representation of what you want to create in your life. Similar to journaling, a vision board helps you keep the vision in front of you.

There are a few different ways to create a vision board. You can create a physical board on poster board. Go through magazines or pictures online for inspiration. Cut or print out images that most align with your vision. Paste them onto the poster board and voilà! You have a vision board.

You can also create a digital vision board. There are a few websites that will allow you to create one for free. You can also use any word or presentation software tool such as Microsoft Word or Microsoft PowerPoint. Again, search through pictures online. Copy and paste those images that most align with your vision onto your digital board. Be mindful of any potential copyright infringements.

There are different trains of thoughts about what to do with the vision board once you have created it. Some people believe that you tuck it away. Some people believe in putting the vision somewhere you can see it every day. I fall into the camp of the latter group. I pinned my physical poster board onto the wall in my office. I also took a picture of it and set it as the background on my cell phone.

It's important to keep the vision in front of you so that you don't forget what you're working toward.

Affirmations

Affirmations are positive statements affirming something that may or may not currently be true but that align with what you want to experience in your life. Most of the time you will see affirmations that start with "I am," such as "I am getting better and better every day."

However, feel free to use any format that resonates with you. One of my favorite affirmations is "Love and blessings are chasing me down."

You can create your own affirmations. You can purchase affirmation tarot cards. You can also just find affirmations online.

I've taken affirmations a step further and created an affirmation board. This is similar to the vision board mentioned previously. However, there are no images, just affirmation cards. My affirmation board is pinned on the wall in my office next to my vision board. I make sure to spend time reading my affirmations and visioning my goals.

Of course you can combine vision and affirmation boards by putting affirmations on your vision board.

Meditation

Meditation is quieting your mind. A quiet mind creates an environment conducive to hearing your intuition more clearly. You can quiet your mind by focusing on your breath, noticing each inhale and exhale. You can use a mantra. You can also focus on a sound or an object.

A lot of people think they can't meditate, but the truth is you meditate all the time. When you have an intense focus on something that eliminates mind chatter, you are in a sense meditating. Showering can be meditative. Receiving a massage can be as well. If you allow your mind to suspend thought and feel the soothing water on your skin or the exhilarating pressure on tight muscles, you can drift into a meditative state. Driving is meditative. Have you ever arrived home without remembering a single landmark, street, or stop sign?

I've provided guided meditations throughout this book. If you think about the words and analyze them, you're not meditating. If you see yourself in the scene without analyzing what's happening, guided meditations are extremely powerful as well.

Quiet Reflection

Quiet reflection is my primary tool for manifesting the life I want. Sometimes the world is so noisy it prevents me from getting and staying in touch with what I'm creating. It's not uncommon to find me sitting in a quiet room for hours, simply reflecting.

Quiet reflection is similar to mediation, but different. When you're meditating, you clear your mind of thoughts. When you're reflecting, you let your thoughts flow. This stream of thought can bring about new desires, ideas, and solutions. Quiet reflection was a major part of writing this book.

These tools help you get clear on what you want and remember what you want so that you can stay consistent. Sometimes when the process takes longer than we anticipated, we lose sight of what we're working toward and why. This is a dangerous place to be. If you don't know where you're going and why, you will venture off the desired path. Leverage these tools to stay on track.

These tools will not help you get what you want absent of action. They are supplementary tools, not the main tool. The main tool is taking consistent action for as long as it takes.

Getting Real

What radical action do you need to take in pursuit of your heart's desires? (If you have no idea, your initial action should be finding out what actions are needed.)

_____
_____
_____

What opportunities are you willing to find and fund for your dream life?

_____
_____
_____

What tools will you experiment with to help you create a life you love?

_____
_____
_____

10 Be Powerful and Confident

It takes a powerful, confident person to transform his or her life into something beautiful. There are so many unknowns, setbacks, and plateaus. It's easy to regress to the life you've always known.

Powerful people prosper. If you want to transform yourself and your life, you have to tap into your powerful self. I've found there are a few key principles that will transform you from powerless to powerful.

Know Who You Are

Imagine Superwoman ignorant to the fact that she has the ability to fly. How powerful would she be in fighting Lex Luthor, her archnemesis, and saving the world?

There's something amazingly special about you. You've always known this to be true. What is it that makes you so special? Don't be afraid to own your gifts. Take hold of them as if they were a million dollars. Your gifts are more precious than money.

You are most powerful when you reach inside yourself and grab the twinkle in your spirit that holds your special powers and light up the world with them. It's not good enough to know your gifts. You have to actually share them.

You'll never be powerful being someone else. You'll never be powerful living out of alignment with the truth of who you are. You will build a breathtaking life, but it won't be your breath taken away. It will be someone else's. You will cringe at the thought of participating in your own life.

If you don't know who you are, you will build someone else's dream life. It will leave you miserable and in despair. No one will understand why your soul is crying. They'll just think you're unappreciative.

Have you heard people say they have a "soul-crushing job" or a "soul-crushing marriage"? You may have uttered those desolate words before yourself. When you're not aligned with who you really are, your soul cries.

I had to write this book to quiet my soul's cries. What do you have to do? What unique gifts do you have to launch into life?

When you don't know who you are, you will continually place yourself smack-dab in the middle of environments that don't fit you. You will surround yourself with the wrong people, the wrong career, and the wrong things in general. You will know that something is off, yet you won't be able to put your finger on it because you don't know who you are.

Who are you?

What do you believe in? What makes you special? What are your strengths and weaknesses? What do you value? What do you stand for or against? What sets your heart on fire? What makes your soul cry? What are your dreams? How do you want the world to see you?

Learning who you are is a process. It's asking yourself questions you may not have asked yourself previously. It's seeing yourself in all your wonder, grace, and magnificence.

Power beyond measure is tucked inside of you. Reach in and grab it by both hands. Proclaim to the world and yourself, "I am powerful."

Know and Ask for What You Want

Clarity is power. Confusion is not. Stop saying you don't know what you want. Your future depends on you knowing. Get clear on what you want from life. Go back to the balance wheel we discussed in chapter 7. If you haven't gotten clear on what you want in each one of those buckets, revisit that exercise.

It's not enough to know what you want. You have to ask for what you want as well. Learning to ask for what I want has been one of my hardest lessons to learn.

Over time, I've learned to ask for what I want unapologetically in every area of my life. I've learned to ask potential suitors to step up. I've learned to ask bosses to allow me to cocreate the role I want to fill on the team. I've learned to ask friends to show up to dinner on time. I grew tired of my needs not being met, so I learned to ask.

And I'm still learning.

There's no power in hoping someone reads your mind.

Protect Your Space

We talked about protecting your space a bit in the chapter on boundaries, but it's worth mentioning here as well.

Remember Marcus, my ex-boyfriend from college? I dated Marcus for five long, painful years. He's not the one who got away. He's the one I let stay for way too long.

"He brings out the worse in me," I confessed to Melissa.

I'd never been much of a curser. Yet with him I was cursing up a storm, arguing, hurling insults, and fussing on a regular basis. My time with him was anything but the peaceful and joyful life attributes I value so much.

I remember talking to my mom one day.

"Is that the way you talk to your mother?" she asked.

I had said something smart and borderline disrespectful. That was the way Marcus talked. I took on his character and his behavior.

Powerful people protect their space like their rib cage protects their heart. When you've allowed someone in your space who is not at the same level as you, it is more likely that you will drop to his or her level. Rarely do we bring people up to our level. Traveling down a flight of stairs is less intensive than traveling up a flight of stairs.

Protect your space. Be mindful of who is in your life and what impact they have on it. Don't let the wrong people in your space. If they happen to manage their way inside your sphere, make sure they don't stay long.

Control Yourself

Powerful people know that their power comes from inside themselves and not from any other person. Some misdirected souls run around trying to control other people. It's easy to fall into the belief that power means controlling others. When you want to feel more powerful, dig deep inside yourself. Pull out your power.

Self-control is power. In other words, being powerful is controlling yourself. It's controlling your emotions. It's controlling your tongue. It's controlling your habits. It's controlling your behavior. It's controlling your thoughts. It's controlling your doubts.

How many times have you let your feelings dictate your behavior?

"I don't feel like exercising."

"I don't feel like washing the dishes."

Stop letting your feelings control your life. Follow your goals, not your feelings. When you follow your goals, your feelings will catch up. They're jealous like that.

It could even be feelings of fear that you find yourself following behind. Your feelings will lead you astray. Your goals, if they're aligned with who you really are, will never lead you astray.

There will always be times when you let your feelings decide your actions for you. As you look to transform your life, get in the habit of choosing your goals and dreams over your feelings more often than not.

Be Present

You are most powerful right here and now. There's no other moment in time that you can influence except the present. If you're not present, it means you are worrying about the future, focused on the past, or living on autopilot. Remember, worry is a low-frequency activity that takes you away from your vision. If you're focused on the past, you're likely bubbling up feelings of anger, sadness, unforgiveness, or regret. These too are low frequency.

Beyond going to the past or future, there's also such a thing as going away mentally. This too prevents people from being present. Alcohol, drugs, excessive TV, and videogames are all things that take you "away."

How can you transform your life if you never want to experience it? How can you close the gap between where you are and where you want to be if you avoid thinking about it? Sure, going "away" helps in the moment. It relieves your disappointments and hurts. In the long run, it does nothing. In fact it actually causes more disappointments and hurts. You'll look at your life and think, "Gosh, I haven't done anything. I haven't accomplished anything. This isn't where I thought I'd be at this point in my life."

That disappointment can lead you deeper into despair. It's a cycle: I don't like my life. I'm stressed and disappointed. Let me take my mind off things. I don't like my life. I'm stressed and disappointed. I'm not where I should be. Let me take my mind off things.

It never ends until you decide to show up and be present. To be present in your life and show up fully, you have to purposefully use your mind to your advantage. Reflect on life. Be honest with yourself. When something pains you, don't try to get rid of the pain as soon as possible. Feel it. Examine it. Learn from it. And then decide what the best path forward is in this moment.

Own Your Results

Powerful people own their results. Time doesn't own their results. Money doesn't own their results. Their spouse doesn't own their results. Their boss doesn't own their results. Nor do their customers.

Powerless people don't take ownership of their results. They blame their less-than-desirable situation on time, money, or other people. Furthermore, they give up way too soon.

If you go to school for three years and one semester, you will not be granted a degree. If you are just one class shy of meeting graduation requirements, it does not matter. You have to stay in it long enough to make it work. If you quit too soon, then it just doesn't work out. Nobody cares if you almost graduated. Excuses are useless. You have to own your results.

It's the same thing with everything in life. If you give up too soon, then you have just essentially dropped out on your dreams. You're a dream dropout. Powerful people don't drop out. They don't give up or stop short of the goal.

How to Own Your Results:

1. Take full responsibility for the outcome. No one or nothing is to blame.
2. Remove obstacles, and find new alternatives.
3. Always be willing to try again.
4. Simple don't give up.

Believe

You are powerful. Your past did not take one ounce of power away from you. It doesn't matter what's in your past. It could be criminal activity, sexual activity, or any other type of activity. All your power is still inside you. No mistake you've ever made has taken it captive. Nothing that anyone has said or done to you has enslaved it.

Your power may have been suppressed for so long it's hard to recognize, but it's still there. Believe in your power. Belief fuels power because it stimulates action. If you don't believe something is possible, you will be reluctant even to try.

So many people have stopped believing. They have reduced life to an experience to get by on. Ask them how they are doing, and you will hear the murmur, "I'm just hanging in there."

But life doesn't want you just hanging on by a thread, dangling in the middle of nowhere. Life wants you to thrive. That's why you were born with all the power you need.

Doubt, suspicions, and fear may have taken over. Disappointments have that effect on us, but we have to resist the urge to allow doubt to flourish. Doubt eclipses power, as do fear and disbelief. Belief spotlights power.

How Do You Believe?

1. You decide to. Make the decision to believe thoughts that feel good and are inspiring to you. Stay away from beliefs that limit you. Limiting beliefs suppress your power. If I didn't believe I could write a book, you wouldn't be reading it right now. If your favorite artist didn't believe in his or her craft, he or she wouldn't be your favorite artist.

2. Search your past for powerful moments. There's a powerful moment in your past. This is a time where you accomplished something you didn't know you could. You helped someone else do something he or she couldn't have done without you. You stood up for something. You shared your gifts. Since your power hasn't gone anywhere, tap into your past powerful moments.

3. Find a proof point. If it's been done before, it can be done again. Find someone who has done what you're believing for.

4. Borrow someone else's belief. If you can't believe in yourself, find someone who does. Let that person's belief in you jumpstart your belief in you. If you can't find someone who believes in you, find someone who has a top-notch belief in themselves. Belief is contagious.

Be Confident

If you're not confident in your power, you'll never acknowledge that it is already tucked inside you ready to beam forth into life. Your confidence needs to be at a healthy level if you want to own your power and walk in it. Here are some easy ways to raise your confidence so that you can walk in your power.

Control Your Thoughts

Confidence is like the cowardly lion. It gets easily scared away by your stinking thinking. Your thoughts can be the biggest deterrent to building confidence. Yes, people can and do plant seeds of inferiority and insignificance in our brains. But then we pull out the fertilizer and water canteen and feed the seeds. Control your thoughts, and starve the self-sabotaging seeds.

When I find myself going down a path of worry or feeling not good enough, I ask myself, "Why are you thinking about that, Charlene?"

This simple question breaks my chain of thought and triggers me to think a new, empowering thought.

Sometimes I'll follow it up with, "What are you thankful for?" or "Why are you good enough?"

We can dwell on a lot of things—our screw-ups, what we think people are saying about us, or what people are actually saying about us. Those thoughts don't serve you. They hurt you. When you control your thoughts, you minimize confidence-killing thoughts.

Find your trigger statement or movement. What can you do or say that will bring notice that you are focusing on the wrong thing and that you should immediately change the thought?

Look the Part

Be Powerful and Confident

I've had a habit of rolling out of bed, throwing something on, and dashing out the door. Some days I have been utterly amazed that I pulled off a decent look. Yet on those days where I was a mess, I felt insecure. You can build your confidence by taking the time to look the part.

Now I know better. I was going to an event one day, and I put on jeans that I didn't like. I forgot that I didn't like them. On the way to the event, I googled the closest clothing store, drove slightly out of the way, purchased a new pair of jeans, and changed in the restroom. Looking and feeling confident is that important. If I don't look the part, I feel insecure. If I feel insecure, I cannot be my powerful authentic self.

The impact of our personal appearance on our confidence levels is often underestimated. Pay attention to what makes you feel confident and at your best. Try to incorporate those things every single day.

Don't wear clothes that are ill-fitting. Whether you lost weight or are going to lose weight, wear clothes that fit and look good on you.

Style your hair in a way that makes you feel confident. You may want to avoid trying new styles when you have an important event to attend. If the new look doesn't turn out the way you thought, you may feel insecure and powerless.

When you're in a funk, you may be inclined to throw anything on, but that makes the funk even worse. Your confidence suffers. Look the part even when you are feeling down. It may even help you feel better.

This is about what makes you authentically feel confident. It's not about what you think should make you feel confident. If you're not sure, start to pay attention to when you feel most confident. Look for trends in your appearance among other factors.

Act the Part

A lot of times we wait for our feelings to rise up first and then our actions to follow. You think that when you feel confident, you'll start to act confident and do things that confident people do. But that's not how it works.

My boss once sent me a meeting invite and asked me to attend in her place. The e-mail invite came through fifteen minutes before the meeting started. It was a meeting with the president of the company who was the number-two person in the entire firm. And here I was the bottom of the totem pole. As I thought about this meeting with high-level executives, I started freaking out a little bit. I felt insecure and had a lack of confidence. My thoughts were enemy number one.

"I don't belong in this meeting with the president," was my initial thought.

Then I gave myself a little pep talk, "Well, Charlene, if you felt like you belonged in this meeting, what would you do?"

I answered myself, "I would walk into the meeting with my head held high. I would walk at a steady pace, not too fast and not too slow. No peeping around the corner like the cowardly lion. I would smile. I would make eye contact. I would introduce myself."

That would be how I would walk into the room if I knew I belonged there. And you know what I did? I walked into the room with my head held high. I had a steady pace. I smiled and spoke to the person sitting next to me. I didn't feel confident, but I was committed to walking in there as though I belonged there.

Sometimes you just have to act the part even though you don't feel the part.

Confidence looks like certain things. I just gave you some of those things. Your head is held high. You're not looking at your feet. You're making eye contact. You're smiling at people. You're speaking up. You're not walking too fast or too slow. You're not slouched over. You're not talking too low; your volume is nice and audible.

You can look confident even if you don't feel confident. Looking confident and acting confident will help you feel confident.

Ease into It

When I go to the beach, I ease into the water because it's so cold. I'll put one foot in first and then slowly ease the rest of my body in. As you look to increase your confidence, baby steps are okay. You don't have to cannonball into confidence. Ease into it in a way that feels comfortable for you, and then keep raising the bar.

Getting Real

Who are you?

_____
_____
_____

What do you want?

_____
_____
_____

How can you look, and act the part to increase your confidence?

_____
_____
_____

Confidence Meditation

Take a deep breath in and exhale. See yourself as the most confident version of yourself.

- What do you look like?
- How do you feel?
- What are you doing?
- What are you saying?
- What are you accomplishing as the most confident version of yourself?

See it play in front of you like a movie. The confident you showing up in your life, in your relationships, in your finances, in your career every single day.

Now, Imagine the most confident version of yourself has even more confidence. What is this new version of confidence doing? Saying? Achieving?

Take this level of confidence and take it up another notch. You are even more confident than your highest level of confidence.

- How are you walking?
- How are you talking?
- How do you feel?
- What are you achieving?
- What are you capable of?
- What are you willing to go after?

Let this feeling permeate all over your body and your mind. Feel the confidence. How is your life different? How are your relationships different?

Download free meditation audio at
fromcaterpillarstobutterflies.com/specialgift

11 Stay the Course

My hope is that what you're learning in this book is the beginning of the end of your current life. I hope the work that you are doing as you read these transformative lessons help usher in a new experience for you; however, I know all too well that there's a natural inclination to start things off really strong. Picking up this book and reading this far is a really great start. Congratulations!

But you also need a really strong finish.

If it is worth starting strong, it is worth ending strong. You picked up this book because you wanted to transform your life, just like the caterpillar does. Yet if you start the transformation and never finish, you'll end up a googly mess with half a wing!

Okay, maybe not a googly mess with half a wing. You will forfeit your dreams and aspirations though. Life won't turn out as breathtaking as you imagined.

It is critical that you have the character, the tenacity, and the resolve to be a strong finisher. That is how you transform your life.

How many times have you started something brand new—a new relationship, a new business, a new workout plan, a new anything—and you started off really strong, and slowly but surely you lost momentum?

I started dating Robert after he stalked me on Facebook. Okay, okay, not quite stalked! We used to work together. We had small talk around the office here and there, but we never interacted much. When I left the company, Robert looked me up on Facebook. That was the beginning.

The first couple of weeks we talked on the phone almost every day. We would talk until one or two o'clock in the morning. If you know me and the way my sleep is set up, you would know it was a miracle that I stayed up that late. We used to instant message throughout the day when we were supposed to be working. We'd meet at the spur of the moment for lunch or a romantic stroll in the park.

Everything was made of sugar and spice and everything nice. Then slowly but surely things started to fizzle out. Instead of late-night chats until the wee hours of the morning, days would go by without talking at all. When we did talk, it was very brief. There were no more last-minute get-togethers. Weeks would go by without even seeing each other.

And then it was over. Strong start. Weak finish.

Stay the Course

So many weight-loss journeys follow this same sad pattern. I've found myself jumping on and off this journey many times myself. Can you relate? You start really strong. You're exercising. You're eating right. You're drinking the amount of water that your body needs, and you're hitting the gym often. You're taking good care of your body and starting to see results. And then you start relaxing. "I'm going to skip today. I'm going to have this cheat meal," you say. Things fall off.

I repeat: if it's worth starting strong, it's definitely worth finishing strong. If it's worth starting to lose weight, then isn't it also worth it to finish losing weight? If it's worth starting your breathtaking transformation, is it not also worth completing it?

I was driving home one evening. It was about five o'clock in the afternoon in the midst of rush-hour traffic. Almeda, the street I travel on my way home, was backed up in a way that was not normal for that particular street. I had to get home because I had a coaching call at six. I didn't want to be late. I decided to take a detour and find another route home.

I veered off the main street and put my home address in my GPS. After a few turns, I ended up back at Almeda, the street that I was originally on. Now I was right past the cause of the traffic backup. There was a four-way intersection, and I saw the lights weren't working. They were all blinking red. Since the lights weren't working, the intersection became a four-way stop. Every car had to stop when they got to the light and let the crossing traffic go. That was causing the backup in traffic.

I was surprised at the magnitude of the impact that it had on traffic. No lanes were closed. There wasn't a car accident. It was just the idea that there was no real forward momentum because every single car had to come to a complete stop. As a result, traffic was stopping and starting, stopping and starting. The street was a parking lot because there was no momentum. There was no green light. There was nothing to get behind.

When you're starting, stopping, starting, and stopping, it backs up your progress. You probably won't even realize the extent, but it is. Commit to a strong finish. Don't peter out at the end only to find yourself having to start all over in a new relationship or a new health regimen.

Get the momentum of the green light on your side so that you can finally get to where you really want to be. Here are seven ways to be a strong finisher.

Finish How You Started

When we start something that we're passionate and hopeful about, we are on fire. We're at the top of our game. We're excited. There's so much enthusiasm. Then somewhere along the line we lose all that excitement, which drives momentum, and we finish very weak, if we finish at all.

One way to finish strong is to end with the beginning in mind. Popular relationship advice says, "Always date your spouse." People who never stop dating their partner understand the value of finishing how you started.

When you first start dating someone, the chemistry and intense connection is hypnotic. All the thoughtful gestures and sweet nothings kindle feelings of love and foreverness. If you stop dating your spouse, then for a lot of couples, the fire is extinguished.

When I am preparing myself for a strong finish, I remind myself of how I started. How many hours did I put in at the start? How many words did I write? How much effort did I put in? Is there an activity that I used to do that fell by the wayside?

If I can finish how I started—when I was at the height of expectancy, faith, and energy—my finish will be spectacular.

When you want to finish strong—or just maintain a strong experience—go back to the beginning. Be that person. Have that level of commitment and desire.

Take it up a Notch

Another way to finish strong is to finish better than you started. We're nearing the end of this book. It is quite possible that you have skipped over all the exercises and Getting Real questions. If you want to finish this book strong by taking it up a notch, you could answer the questions and play full out.

When you are committed to finishing strong, ask yourself, "What else can I be doing?"

Turn the heat up. Play full out. Finish stronger than you started.

Have a Plan

I was listening to a good friend of mine and business owner do a talk online about finishing the year strong. Her advice for finishing strong was to make sure you have a plan. She was speaking specifically about finishing the year strong, but I think this advice holds true no matter what you are finishing. Have a plan for what you're going to do next. Know what you're going to do once you've accomplished your goal. Decide in advance what you're going to do for the next year or for the next phase of the journey that you're on.

For example, you have worked really hard to get to your goal weight. You're almost there. What are you going to do once you are there? Eat whatever you want to eat? Cut back your gym schedule?

Know what's next so that you don't lose the progress you've made. When you have a plan for what's next, you are setting yourself up for further success.

Have Discipline

When you're disciplined, you can go nearly anywhere you want to go. Discipline is about sticking with the right actions long enough to see results. The rigor of committing to the right activities day in and day out for as long as you need to will guarantee you finish strong.

The best way to have discipline is to set a schedule and stick to it. Have a schedule for working out. Have a schedule for waking up. Have a schedule for everything. When you have a schedule, you remove the self-sabotaging mechanism called decisioning.

"Should I work out today or tomorrow? I guess I'll work out tomorrow. It's raining today."

When you give yourself room to make a decision, you might not make the best decision for your future. When you set a schedule that is most aligned with where you want to go and you don't give yourself space to wiggle out of it by "decisioning," your finish will be strong.

Have an Inspiring Routine

This is along the same lines as having discipline, but I wanted to talk about routines separately. You may have heard a lot about creating morning routines. There's a lot of talk online about how successful, famous people start the day.

As much as I have heard the value of creating a morning (and evening) routine, my attitude was always "Meh." And then I realized I do have a morning routine. I get up. I use the restroom. I take the dog out. There is a specific set of activities I do in the morning generally in a specific order.

You likely already have morning and evening routines as well. The key is to incorporate activities that are inspiring and supportive of what you want to create in your life.

You don't have to overhaul your morning routine tomorrow. You can gradually ease things in. When I decided to intentionally create an inspiring morning routine, the first thing I did was incorporate gospel music. Then I added in journaling and so forth.

FROM CATERPILLAR TO BUTTERFLY

If you want to overhaul your morning routine tomorrow, go for it! If that feels overwhelming and you are likely to put it off, introduce one new inspiring, supportive activity tomorrow.

Having the right routines to start and end your day can help you be a strong finisher.

Some ideas to get you started are below. You can incorporate these in either the morning or evening:

- Pray.
- Listen to inspiring music.
- Listen or read inspirational videos, books (physical books, e-books, or audio books), sermons, seminars, podcasts, or blogs.
- Read a daily devotional.
- Write your goals down.
- Write a letter to yourself.
- Read past letters to yourself.
- Journal.
- Go for a walk.
- Meditate.
- Perform quiet reflection.
- Visualize your ideal future.
- Exercise.
- Shower.

The idea is that you create a routine that feels good to you and puts you in the best state of being (mentally, physically, spiritually, and emotionally) to help you live and create the life you want to create. If taking a shower helps you feel invigorated and energized, you may want to take showers in the morning before you start your day. If meditating calms you, you may want to meditate at night to lead you into sleep so that you can be well rested the next day.

Create routines that inspire you, support you, and equip you with what you need to accomplish, to create a life you love.

Always Get Back Up

It's likely that you will fall. You will jump off the bandwagon. You will stop and start over and over again. When that happens, get back up. If you still want what you want, then don't settle. Get back at it as soon as you can.

Sometimes we fall and stay down. The longer you stay down, the harder it is to get back up. Don't let a hiccup completely throw you off. Always get back up and get back up quickly.

Have a Support System

Lastly you can finish strong by surrounding yourself with people who are on that same journey or who can support you on that journey. You need someone who isn't going to let you get off the hook. Or you want to have a network of people who are on the same journey with you who can also help you finish.

If you're starting a business, then be around other business owners. If you are losing weight, be around other people who are losing weight or who already have the healthy habits that you want to adopt. Staying connected to an inspiring support system that will keep you accountable is great way to make sure that you finish strong.

What Happens When You Get Stuck?

I believe in my heart of hearts that we can create the life that we want. It won't be a perfect life. Everything won't go according to plan, but I just believe that what I want is available to me. And what you want is available to you. It is heartbreaking for me to see people live below their potential and stay in a place of being stuck.

I want to walk up to every person who feels stuck and say, "Why are you staying stuck? Come on! Let's go!"

But I can't; however, I can give you a really great tip on how you can move forward if you find yourself stuck. There are many ways to get unstuck. This is one of the most powerful ways because it doesn't require anyone or anything special except for you.

Get unstuck by doing what you can. There is always something you can do. Even when you feel stuck, if you really think about it, there's always something within your control.

If you're stuck in your career, have been applying for a new job to no avail for months, there is still something else you could do. You could still apply again to open positions. You can still update your résumé.

Even when you feel as though you've exhausted all your options, there is always something you can do. There is always someone you can call. There is always something within your capacity to control.

When you believe that there is nothing you can do, you have placed yourself in a hopeless situation. Instead of putting yourself in a position of empowerment, you're stifling yourself. Get the notion out of your head that there is nothing you can do, because there really is always something you can do.

You might not want to do what there is to do. You might feel that you have done it a couple billion times already, but there is still always something else you can do.

Several years ago I was fired from my job. I happened to be interviewing with another company at the time. Between the first interview and the second interview, I was fired. I never mentioned this tidbit to the new company. They extended an offer, and I accepted it. Part of the onboarding process was verifying all the past employers I had listed on my application. My soon-to-be-new employer sent an employment verification request to the old employer.

My old employer—the one who fired me—drug their feet with returning the verification form. I was really stressed. I was stressed because I didn't know what they were going to say. I didn't know if they were the type of company that only verified dates of employment and title or if they would actually say that I was fired. To add to it, they were taking forever to fill out the employment verification, which was stressing me out further. That measly sheet of paper was the only thing standing between me, a steady paycheck, and health insurance. Actually, to say I was stressed would have been an understatement. I was beyond stressed and frazzled for days waiting on the form to be returned to my would-be employer.

I was unemployed. I had no income. I had no health care. I had no other options. I needed this job. If it fell through, I had to start all over again. Finding a job from applying to interviewing to checking references could take months. I felt stuck and helpless.

"What are they over there doing? What's wrong with these people?" I wondered on the hour every hour every day, day after day.

And then suddenly the thought occurred to me. "Just call them."

And so I did. I explained I was due to start my new job as soon as they completed the necessary paperwork. The woman on the other end of the line was very friendly and understanding. She said she saw my form in the bin and would put it on top of the pile.

Immediately I felt relieved. I didn't get to start the job the next Monday. My start date was still pushed back. They did say I was fired. I had to have my references checked, but I was no longer sitting there helpless at the mercy of someone else.

The fact that I had called and at least moved the process along immediately relieved me. I immediately felt unstuck. I immediately felt less anxious. I was able to enjoy the next few days of being unemployed instead of walking around stressful about it. I did what I could do to move the situation forward.

There is always something you can do to get yourself unstuck. There is something that doesn't depend on anyone other than you. There is always someone you can call, something you can read, or an e-mail you can send. If you're always doing the one thing that is within your control to do, you'll always manage to get unstuck.

Getting Real

How can you take your transformation up a notch?

_____
_____
_____

What's your plan for what's next (after you've completed this book)?

_____
_____
_____

What can you do right now to move an area of your life forward?

_____
_____
_____

12 Rules for the Journey

A recurring theme in this book has been the inspiring truth that life is a journey. Not only is life a journey, but it is comprised of a series of journeys we get to experience and travel. As you prepare to embark on the next leg of your journey, keep these rules of the road in mind.

Avoid the Parking Lot

If you're not prepared for the journey, you're not going to make it. I want you to make it. I want you to be successful in creating the life you want to create.

"Charlene, how do I get from Houston to Florida?" Maury inquired.

"Get on I-10. It's a straight shot. Just a few hours," I answered.

And with that Maury got in his car and jumped on I-10 to make his way from Houston to Florida.

"It's just a few hours," he thought. "I'll be there in no time."

The problem is it's not just a few hours. It might not even be a straight shot.

This isn't a true story, but imagine I gave those simple directions to Maury. He wouldn't be prepared for the journey. He might not have enough gas to get there.

When I moved from Tallahassee, Florida, to Houston, it was a ten-hour drive. If Maury wanted to go to South Florida, such as Miami, he might need to spend the night somewhere and pick up the next day. He might not have enough money, gas, or time to get there because I didn't tell him the whole story.

As a coach I have the duty and responsibility to let you know what you're in for so that you can withstand the setbacks and obstacles. I want you to have enough gas in your gas tank. I want you to have enough grit and perseverance. You need to have enough prayer, inspiration, and energy to sustain you on the journey.

Most people think accomplishing a dream is equivalent to going two blocks up the road, turning left, going up one stoplight, and finding the dream on the right. In fact, it's not uncommon for coaches, trainers, and business marketers to tell prospects that very thing.

And the ambitious souls will go there, but they won't see the vision. They won't see the dream. They will think, "Maybe I got it wrong. Maybe I misunderstood." They will go wandering around to see if they can find it. Then they'll come across a parking lot.

Rules for the Journey

    Many people will be in the parking lot. The dream seekers will say to themselves, "Someone over there in that parking lot has got to know where my dream is." And they will head over to the parking lot.

    The dreamers will pull up to the first person they see and say, "Hey, I'm trying to find my dream. I can't find it. I was told it was two blocks up the street, turn left, go to the next stoplight, turn right, and it will be there. It's not there. Can you help me?"

    A small smirk will appear on the person's face as he or she answers, "Sweetheart, there is no dream. You see all these cars here? You see all these people hanging out here in the parking lot? If there was a dream, they wouldn't all be here. But they're all here because they thought the same thing you're thinking. They were told the same thing that you were told. It's a lie. Just relax. Kick your feet up. Have some beer and pizza. Watch a movie on the big screen. Nothing else is out there for you. This is as good as it gets."

    Most people will reply, "You know what? You're right. I've been wandering around trying to find this dream forever, and I really could use a beer."

    A very selected few will say, "Hey, I hear you. I hear you, but I just can't shake the feeling that the dream is out there somewhere." These brave, courageous souls will turn out of the parking lot and keep looking for the dream.

    They'll wander around some more on the streets of life. After spending some time trying to retrace their steps and get to the dream, they'll come to another parking lot. And again they will say to themselves,

"Someone in there has got to know where the dream is."

They'll pull over into that parking with less excitement and more discouragement than the first. "Hey, guys. I'm trying to find my dream. I was told it was around here somewhere. Can you help me?"

"You're funny," the dream doubter will laugh. "What dream? Get off your high horse. Get out of the clouds. Look at all these people here. You think if there was a dream out there all these people would be in here drinking margaritas and eating popcorn? You dreamers are so funny. Nothing else is out there for you. Just sit down. Watch a movie on the big screen. Have a margarita and some popcorn. Trust me, it's a lot of fun here," they will say convincingly.

You'll glance around and see everyone socializing. It doesn't *seem* so bad in the parking lot.

The dream doubter will continue, "You go out there, and you're going to get lost or stuck. You're going to be on the side of the road with no gas. Plus, it's lonely out there. Just chill here. The dream doesn't exist."

Yet again most of those who wind up at the second parking lot will say, "You know what? I'm just going to take a break. I'll have one margarita and a handful of popcorn. Then after that I'll start looking for my dream again."

There's a funny thing about breaks. Sometimes they end up lasting for years. Other times they last indefinitely.

Again there will be a slight few who will say to the dream doubter, "Ah! What you're saying makes sense. There *are* a lot of people here. They *do* seem to be having fun. I could enjoy a margarita, but I *just* can't shake this feeling. I just can't shake the feeling that my dream is out there somewhere, and I wouldn't be able to live with myself if I didn't go out and try."

Which person will you be? The one who stays at the first parking lot? Or will you fight the first bout of discouragement and frustration and make it to the second parking lot only to settle there? Or will you be one of the select few who refuse to stop in the parking lots of life on the way to their dream?

Trying to accomplish any great feat requires grit. It is further than what you think it is. And there are a lot of people who have parked in a parking lot on the side of the road who have given up. They have convinced themselves that nothing is out there. They have surrounded themselves with other people who are also convinced nothing is out there. When everybody's telling you that achieving your dreams is impossible their perspective can rub off on you. Don't let that happen. Don't end up in the parking lot of life.

Your dream life is not two blocks up the street, turn to the left, go up to the next stoplight, and it's on the right. Here's what it really looks like:

Go two blocks up the street. Turn right. Go up to the next stoplight and make a left. Go all the way down that street until you can't go on anymore. It's a dead-end. You're going to have to go right or left. I don't know which way you should go. I can't decide that for you, but you've got to go right or left. Make a decision.

No matter which way you go, you're going to go down another long, boring road and end up in a valley. You're going to go way down into that valley. It's going to get dark. You're going to be alone. You may even become afraid. It is also very likely that you will hear weird noises.

You don't want to give up in the valley. Keep going through it. If you keep going you will come out the other side. Once you've made it out you will go down another long, boring road. You'll get to the end of that road and realize you're lost. Make a U-turn. Come back around the other way. Then take a right.

If you keep going and going *and going*, you're going to come to the base of a mountain. You have to make your way up the mountain for there lies your dream. At some point when climbing up the mountain, you're going to realize that you can't go with your car anymore. Get out and hike it up the rest of the way. But keep going.

You'll see some people who are there on the mountain. They haven't reached the top, but they're just hanging out on the mountain. Many settled somewhere along the way. You'll be tempted to settle too. You might hear the faint voice of a well-meaning person tell you that no one has ever made it to the top: "This is as far as you can go."

Don't listen to that person. Keep hiking your way to the top of the mountain. When you get to the top, you will look around at your accomplishment. You will feel a sense of confidence and pride that no one can take away from you. As you look around marveling in the beauty of the scenic view, you will notice that there are bigger, better mountains that you will also wish to climb.

That is what it really looks like accomplishing your goals and transforming your life. If you pull over into the parking lot, you will never catch even a glimpse of all that is available and waiting for you.

Don't Worry about How Long It Takes

If there is a space in the world or your life that you see, and you know you can fill that space, it doesn't matter how long it's going to take. Stop holding yourself hostage to a time line.

What if Dr. Martin Luther King Jr. had said, "This is taking too long. I give up"?

What if there were cancer researchers and doctors who said, "This is hopeless. I give up"? That would be crazy, right?

We wouldn't have so many of the things that we have today. You have to decide for yourself that you're not going to give up. Make a commitment to yourself right now that you will not hold your dreams hostage to a time line that someone made up for you or that you made up for yourself. Forget the time line. Fill the space in your life, in your heart, in your community, and in your industry. Fill the space in the world that needs to be filled. And don't let it matter how long it takes. Don't be obsessed with time. Forget time.

Never Stop Believing

Creating a life you love is possible. You're not asking for too much. You're not being greedy or selfish. You're being you. If your heart dreamed up a better life than the one you have, it is your duty to follow your heart. Never stop believing in yourself or your vision. Hold to it tight. It's more than possible. You are worthy and capable of bringing your dreams about.

Celebrate and Honor Yourself

FROM CATERPILLAR TO BUTTERFLY

My mastermind sister once called me "modest Charlene." It's true. I always say, "I only" or "I just" when it comes to something I've accomplished. In my head I have *so* far to go. What's there to celebrate?

But celebrating feels good, and it's good for you. Not only is it good for you; it's good for all the people who are a little bit behind you as well. Sometimes we're so focused on who's ahead of us and how far we have to go that we forget about those who are following behind us, watching us. We should celebrate ourselves and share our victories for those people too.

You should celebrate yourself because you're the first in line to celebrate and cheer for someone else. You should celebrate yourself because if anyone deserves your praise and adulation, it's you!

So don't forget to celebrate yourself. For what?

~ Making it this far in life
~ Picking up this book and working through the exercises
~ Having enough faith to take a chance on something that can change the trajectory of your life
~ Believing in yourself and your dreams
~ Pushing through whatever walls you had to push through (and I know you pushed through at least one wall in recent times)

You don't have to wait for the big moments in life to celebrate. You are accomplishing feats every single day. Every day you could crumble, give in, give up, and show out. But instead, you persevere. You keep charging toward all that you know life can be. You maintain your character and integrity in a world full of the opposite.

You show up again and again and are always willing to try just one more time.

And for that celebrate who you are.

As you reflect on this last week or month of your life, think of how you can celebrate and honor yourself—you're worth it. Life is lived in the small moments, not the big ones, so you should celebrate in the small ones. Small moments of celebration could give you the energy and resolve to keep going. It's beneficial to stop and acknowledge how far you have come on a consistent basis. Celebrating your victories is an important part of your journey.

Don't forget or neglect to celebrate yourself. You rock! You deserve it. You need it.

And as you stop to celebrate all that you are and are becoming, know that I celebrate you too!

I celebrate you for believing enough in yourself to pick up this book. I celebrate you for making it this far. I celebrate you for being courageous enough to embark on a journey to transform yourself and your life.

Get Support

I've said before you're not going to be able to transform your life completely on your own. You will need support. All the greats—musicians, actors, businesspeople—have learned under the wing of someone else. It's an important part of the journey.

The biggest advantage of having a coach, mentor, or guide is the accountability. The American Society of Training and Development (ASTD) published a study that said when you have an appointment scheduled with an accountability partner, the likelihood of you accomplishing a task or a goal increases to 95 percent. Because when we are holding ourselves accountable, it's very easy not to follow through. But when we know that we have to answer to someone else, we tend to button up really quickly.

I attended a leadership conference over the course of multiple days. At the end of day one, we were given a homework assignment. The assignment was to tell someone that we love them. With no pretense or special reason, just say to them, "I love you."

I went home that night, and I did not do my homework. The next morning, I was less than a mile away from the hotel where the conference was hosted. I picked up my cell phone and called my mom. Before I walked into the conference, I said, "Hey, Mom, I just called to say I love you."

Why? Because I could not go into this conference with this coach and all these other participants and say I didn't do my homework. I *had* to do my homework. Even if we do our assignment at the last possible second while we were walking in the door, the likelihood that we are going to do what we said we were going to do increases to the ninety-fifth percentile when someone is holding us accountable.

Another benefit of having support is you have a safe space to release what's been mellowing in your head and heart. Sometimes we need to be heard, but that opportunity isn't always available in our day-to-day lives. We need to talk through whatever it is we're up against to gain clarity, peace, or just the satisfaction of truly being seen and heard.

At the end of a coaching session, my client Ivy said to me, "I can't believe I talked so much. I never talk this much. I can't believe I was so open. I never share anything."

When someone's listening to you and holding a space for you to say what needs to be said and think through what you need to think through, it's a powerful experience. When you are heard and not judged but invited to express yourself, sometimes you just can't stop talking. We are not heard a lot of the time. We go through life without ever being fully seen or fully heard. We bottle up a lot, and sometimes we burst. Within the confides of a safe coaching relationship, you can say the things that you can't say to anybody else. You can be fully seen and fully heard.

Bridget and I would have a call once a week. One week she would say she was working on a particular project. The next week she would say she's working on two new projects.

I would exclaim, "Hold up, Bridget! What about the project you were working on last week?? Did you finish it yet?"

"No."

"Why are you working on two new projects if you have not finished the last one?"

We all have our quirks and weaknesses. Some people like Bridget are great at starting things and not so great at finishing things. She may have never realized that about herself before us working together. Having an accountability partner helps keep you on the right track. It can help you circumvent the self-sabotaging parts of your character. Bridget sabotaged herself by starting a thousand tasks related to her goals and finishing none.

Other times we know what we need to do, but we just don't do it. This is another way we sabotage ourselves. Whether we're waiting on permission from someone else or on our confidence to increase, we sit on our ideas.

This is what happened with Denise. She shared with me a great idea during our coaching call. At the time she was unemployed and finding it difficult to secure a job. She had toyed with the idea of starting her own marketing consulting business and had even done similar work in the past. For whatever reason she hesitated to take action on her new idea. Ideas alone are useless.

"Well, what can you do about it?" I asked Denise.

"I know two people who could probably use my services," she replied.

"So if you know these people who can use your services, then what should you do about that? What *can* you do about that?"

Denise answered, "I could reach out to them and share my idea with them to see if they are interested."

"Okay, great. By when?" I prompted.

"By Friday."

"Okay. So you will reach out to these two people by Friday. How are you going to do it? Are you going to e-mail them? Are you going to call them?"

"I could probably call Susie. I know her very well, but I'll send John an e-mail."

"Okay, great. So by this Friday you're going to call Susie and send John an e-mail about your business idea, right?"

"Yeah. Okay. I can do that." Denise said hesitantly.

"Okay, great. When you get it done, send me a text message."

That's literally how the conversation went. She already knew what to do. She already had the idea. I didn't give it to her, but I helped her move along to make progress. I helped her get out of her head just by asking her a few questions and asking her to put a deadline on it. And sure enough, I received a text message from her that Friday saying she reached out to Susie and John. That's the power of coaching and mentoring. Your to-do list gets done.

You will need support on the journey to transforming your life. It may take the form of an accountability partner, someone to listen to you, or a coach. Get the support you need. Don't be afraid to ask for help. Again it's an important part of the journey and can keep you out of the parking lot.

Getting Real

How committed are you to avoiding the parking lot where dreams go to die? Why?

_____
_____
_____

Why do you believe in yourself and your vision?

_____
_____
_____

What support will you get along the way?

_____
_____
_____

13 Conclusion

You are more than equipped to transform the life you have into the life you want. It's easy to believe that your situation is hopeless. "These are just the cards I've been dealt," you might say.

I get it. You may not have been born with a silver spoon in your mouth. Maybe your household wasn't a healthy, loving environment. Maybe your parents didn't give you what you needed or instill empowering beliefs into you.

Yes, life seemingly deals some better hands than others.

In the game of spades, once all the cards are dealt, each player assesses the cards received. If any player has zero spades, they are allowed to throw the hand in. They are allowed to ask for the cards to be redealt. You can't play spades without spades.

You too can ask for a new hand. I believe in reading this book and making it this far, that is exactly what you have done. You have asked life to reshuffle the deck and give you a better hand.

Life will oblige. There are many rags-to-riches stories. People from all walks of life have conquered pasts and created better futures. You can do the same.

The truth is you don't want your life to be easy. You don't want to pass the finish line without breaking a sweat. You want to be the runner who pushes harder than ever before. You want to crawl through the finish line, sweating, out of breath, and crying tears of joy. You want the crowd to take a collective inhale and then rise from their seats to witness your triumph.

You think you want it easy, but that wouldn't make you remarkable.

I heard a story of a man walking through a park. He spotted a butterfly on the ground still inside its cocoon. The butterfly was struggling to break free. The well-intentioned man bent down and cut the butterfly out of the cocoon.

This sounds like a good thing, but it wasn't. The butterfly needed to hit its wings against the cocoon to strengthen them. By removing the obstacle, the man weakened the butterfly.

You don't want it to be easy. You want to face life head on. You want to learn what you're made of.

Accomplishing feats I didn't feel prepared to accomplish has given me confidence and fulfillment I have never

Conclusion

known. I became a bit more unstoppable. Achieving the impossible is the best way to build your confidence and put you on the path to conquer even more.

Personal Growth Plan

When accomplishing your dreams isn't easy, it means you have to grow. I'm a big fan of having a personal growth plan. Knowing where you need to grow and how to grow is powerful.

There's always a gap between where you are and where you want to be. Having a personal growth plan will help you close the gap. Here's a four-step process for how you can create a plan that will facilitate your growth.

Step 1: Start with where you are. You likely have already started to paint the picture of what your current situation is and where you are dissatisfied.

Some questions to reflect on are below:

- What's your current situation?
- How do you feel?
- Where are you dissatisfied?
- Where are you satisfied?

Step 2: Next you want to paint a picture of what you want your future to look like. Revisit chapter 6, where you defined your vision.

Some questions to reflect on for step 2:

- What are your goals?
- Where do you see yourself in three, five, or ten years?
- What have you always wanted to do?
- How do you want to show up in the world?

- What's missing in your life?

Step 3: Cement why you must close the gap now. If you don't feel that it is absolutely necessary to close the gap between where you are and your vision, you probably won't close it. If you don't believe that the gap must be closed right now, then you are likely to put it off for another day or another year.

Questions to reflect on for step 3:
- On a scale of one to ten, ten being the highest, how bad do you want to close the gap?
- What will life be like if you close the gap?
- Who else needs you to close the gap?
- What will life be like if you never close the gap?
- On a scale of one to ten, ten being the highest, how committed are you to closing the gap at this time in your life?

Step 4: Identify what is needed to close the gap. Anytime there is a gap (I said previously that there is always a gap), it means that something is missing on the individual's part. If we had everything we needed, there wouldn't be a gap.

Filling the gap requires something new from you. This might include experience, skill, knowledge, habits, beliefs, time, support, energy, commitment, desire, or coaching.

What do you need to close the gap? Be specific. If you need new knowledge, specify exactly what new knowledge you need.

How will you close the gap? Will you read a book or take a course? Again, be

Conclusion

specific. Specify the exact book(s) you will read to close the knowledge gap.

When will you close the gap? Don't let this linger forever. If you know that there is an area in which you need to grow and you've identified how to grow, put a date on it. Stick to the date.

That's it. That is how you create a personal growth plan so that you can grow in the way you most need to grow to get you to where you most want to go. You can find a personal growth plan to complete on page 208.

Final Thoughts

At any given time, you can make a new decision. You can make a decision that is completely different than every other decision you have made up until this point. Your past does not equate your future. You can transform from a caterpillar to butterfly.

Not only *can* you transform, you *should* transform. Even if you have to crawl across the finish line, you should make your life as captivating as you can.

If you still have doubts about what's possible for you or believe you don't deserve a better life, move forward anyhow. Let the *future you* prove the *current you* wrong. Taking a leap of personal growth and courage is indicative of more than any material gain or prestigious honor.

It's a sign that you love yourself enough to be your best self. It's a sign that you forgive yourself for the times you screwed up, the dumb decisions you've made, and the ways you acted outside your best interests. You give yourself grace for the times you let you down.

FROM CATERPILLAR TO BUTTERFLY

When you're willing to move past where you are and where you've been, it's a statement of faith in God, yourself, and every person who saw something in you that you didn't even see inside yourself.

This is bigger than just vacations and cars. This is about purpose, potential, fulfillment, and love. You were meant to transform. You are not meant to stay the same. You will not fully embrace how true that statement is until you allow yourself to build a cocoon of love-infused growth around you and come out the other side a masterpiece.

Here's to your growth.

Appendix and Worksheets

FROM CATERPILLAR TO BUTTERFLY

Life Balance Wheel
Current Situation

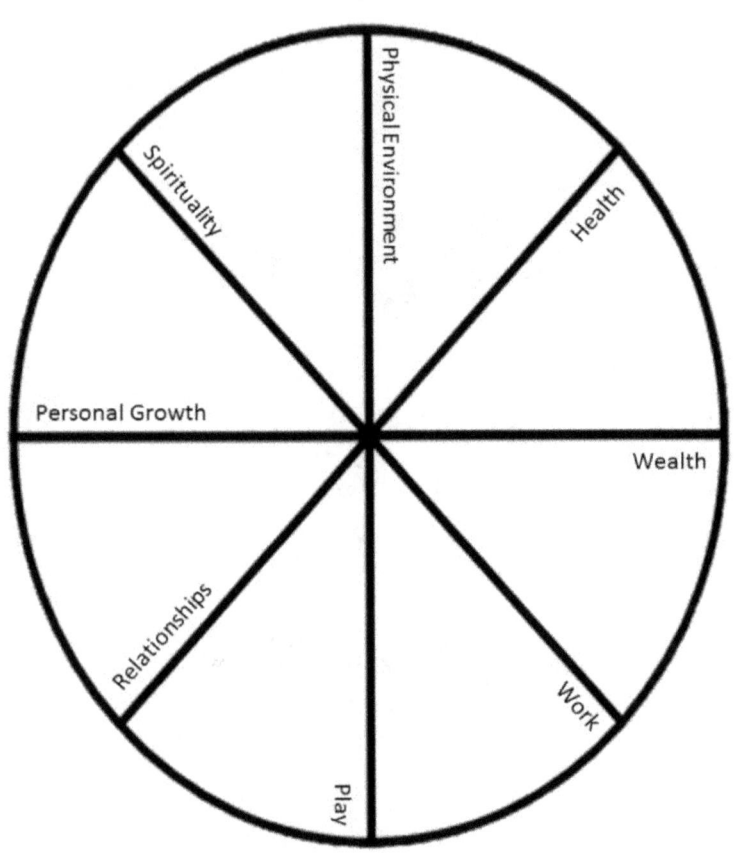

Appendix and Worksheets

Life Balance Wheel
Desired Situation

- Physical Environment
- Health
- Wealth
- Work
- Play
- Relationships
- Personal Growth
- Spirituality

FROM CATERPILLAR TO BUTTERFLY

Boundaries

Things I say yes to:	Things I say no to:

Appendix and Worksheets

Core Values List

Achievement	Imagination	Purity	Strength
Appreciation	Impact	Recognition	Success
Authenticity	Independence	Reliability	Support
Balance	Inner Harmony	Religion	Sympathy
Clarity	Integrity	Reputation	Synergy
Closeness	Intelligence	Resilience	Thoughtfulness
Comfort	Intimacy	Resourcefulness	Timeliness
Commitment	Intuition	Respect	Tranquility
Communication	Joy	Responsibility	Transcendence
Dependability	Kindness	Sacredness	Trustworthiness
Discipline	Knowledge	Satisfaction	Truth
Education	Liveliness	Security	Understanding
Experience	Love	Self-control	Uniqueness
Faith	Loyalty	Selflessness	Unity
Fearlessness	Maturity	Self-realization	Usefulness
Fidelity	Meaningful Work	Self-reliance	Warmth
Flexibility	Mindfulness	Self-Respect	Wealth
Freedom	Moderation	Sensitivity	Willingness
Friendships	Openness	Sensuality	Wisdom
Frugality	Order	Service	Worthiness
Generosity	Organization	Sharing	Zest
Genuineness	Originality	Significance	
Gratitude	Passion	Silence	
Growth	Peace	Simplicity	
Happiness	Perseverance	Sincerity	
Harmony	Philanthropy	Solidarity	
Health	Playfulness	Solitude	
Honesty	Pleasure	Sophistication	
Humility	Preparedness	Spirituality	
Humor	Presence	Stability	
	Privacy	Stillness	
	Prosperity		

FROM CATERPILLAR TO BUTTERFLY

Level Up Your Day to Day

	Current Experience
Shopping	
Where you shop for groceries	
Where you shop for clothes	
Vacation & Entertainment	
Where you vacation	
How often you vacation	
What you do for entertainment	
What you read for fun	
Meals	
What you eat at home	
Where you eat when eating out	
What you order when eating out	
Mindset	
Your first thought of the day	
Your last thought of the day	
People You Associated With	
Friends	
Family	
Coworkers	
Other	

Appendix and Worksheets

Level Up Your Day to Day

	LevelUp Experience
Shopping	
Where you shop for groceries	
Where you shop for clothes	
Vacation & Entertainment	
Where you vacation	
How often you vacation	
What you do for entertainment	
What you read for fun	
Meals	
What you eat at home	
Where you eat when eating out	
What you order when eating out	
Mindset	
Your first thought of the day	
Your last thought of the day	
People You Associated With	
Friends	
Family	
Coworkers	
Other	

FROM CATERPILLAR TO BUTTERFLY

Personal Growth Plan

	How Will	
Where I Need to Grow	Learn	Read
1.	By: __/__	
2.	By:	
3.	By:	
4.	By:	
5.	By:	

Appendix and Worksheets

Personal Growth Plan

I Grow?			
Attend	Invest in	Speak to	Other

Going Deeper

I hope that what you've learned in this book has led to a personal breakthrough for you. Yet I know that it's not enough. If you want to create momentum behind your transformation and go a little deeper here are some additional resources to support you.

❧ Private One-on-One Coaching with me, Charlene

Receive personalized coaching on the principles taught in this book and how to apply to your life specifically.

fromcaterpillarstobutterflies.com/coaching

❧ Transform Your Year Planner

You transform your life one year at a time. This planner will help you transform your year so you can transform your life.

fromcaterpillarstobutterflies.com/year

❧ Transform Your Relationship Planner

Relationships of all kinds are a big part of life. Take your relationship from failing to thriving.

fromcaterpillarstobutterflies.com/relationship

❧ Transform Your Wealth: Real Estate Investing 101

I added $28,000 to my net worth and $400 to my monthly income with one house. Take this introductory course to learn the basics of single family real estate investing.

fromcaterpillarstobutterflies.com/wealth

About Charlene

Charlene Dior Blandon is founder of fromcaterpillarstobutterflies.com, a site dedicated to self-development and transformation. Charlene is an award winning speaker, trainer and coach based in Houston, TX. She holds certifications in coaching and self-hypnosis and mindfulness meditation.

Charlene is known for being a woman of big vision that influences those around her to expand their vision as well. She speaks and trains on expanding your vision to expand your life or business. Charlene also provides transformational coaching for women who feel they are living below their potential so that they can live the highest vision they have for themselves and their families.

In addition to her transformation work, Charlene also dabbles in real estate investing. She is an avid traveler having visited London, Paris, Rome, Brazil, Thailand, and Honduras to name a few. Charlene is passionate about building wealth and experiences and helping others to do the same.

"Be Really You" is her personal motto. "Not just a little bit of you. Not just some of the time. All of you, all of the time." Charlene believes that when you embrace the real you and strive toward your highest vision, you will transform your life from a caterpillar to a butterfly.

For speaking inquiries, media inquiries, or questions about online courses and personalized coaching please email her at Charlene@fromcaterpillarstobutterflies.com.

Special Gift

Download audio of all three meditations featured in this book. It is my way of saying thank you. Each guided meditation is set to handpicked, inspiring music to enhance your experience. All you have to do is tell me what email address you'd like me to send your complimentary meditations to!

Visit
fromcaterpillarstobutterflies.com/specialgift

Offer subject to change or be discontinued. Not redeemable for cash.

Listen to the Podcast!

Just like the caterpillar is destined to become a butterfly, you too are designed for a beautiful transformation. This is where you go to grow and transform your life.

Learn life changing principles and be inspired to reach your fullest potential. Hosted by author and coach, Charlene Dior Blandon.

Find the show on iTunes, Stitcher, GooglePlay, and Podbean.

www.ingramcontent.com/pod-product-compliance
Lightning Source LLC
LaVergne TN
LVHW051116080426
835510LV00018B/2065